To Natalee,

Keep writing – it's a
recipe for success.

A RECIPE FOR SUCCESS

Other Badger Biographies

A RECIPE FOR SUCCESS

Lizzie Kander and Her Cookbook

BY BOB KANN

WISCONSIN HISTORICAL SOCIETY PRESS

Published by the Wisconsin Historical Society Press
Publishers since 1855

wisconsin**history**.org

All artifacts photographed by Joel Heiman unless otherwise indicated. On page 62, Dover egg beater is WHS Museum 1974.240.48; double boiler is WHS Museum 1973.60.47; and angel food cake pan is WHS Museum 1964.14.4.

Photographs identified with PH, WHi, or WHS are from the Society's collections; address inquiries about such photos to the Visual Materials Archivist at the above address.

Printed in the United States of America
Cover design by Nancy Zucker
Text design by Jill Bremigan

13 12 11 10 09   2 3 4 5 6

Library of Congress Cataloging-in-Publication Data
Kann, Bob.
 A recipe for success : Lizzie Kander and her cookbook / by Bob Kann.
    p. cm.
 Includes index.
 ISBN-13: 978-0-87020-373-2 (pbk. : alk. paper)
 ISBN-10: 0-87020-373-8 (pbk. : alk. paper)
1. Kander, Simon, Mrs.–Juvenile literature. 2. Food writers–Wisconsin–Milwaukee–Biography–Juvenile literature. I. Title.
 TX649.K36K36 2006
 641.5092–dc22
 [B]
                    20060169

Front cover: Portrait courtesy of Milwaukee Jewish Historical Society. Back cover: Photo courtesy of Milwaukee County Historical Society.

∞ The paper used in this publication meets the minimum requirements of the American National Standard for Information Sciences—Permanence of Paper for Printed Library Materials, ANSI Z39.48-1992.

This book is dedicated to my mother and my father. You always made sure there was good food on the table and love in our home that I could count on.

Lizzie B. Kander

Contents

Cookbook covers from 1954, 1936, 1915, and 1901

Introduction
Meet Lizzie Kander

How many cooks does it take to screw in a light bulb?
One, but she has to have the right recipes to do it.

What does it take to change the lives of millions of people? Inventing something like the light bulb or the computer? A magic wand? Not always. Lizzie Kander did it with a cookbook. It was a very special cookbook, though. All cookbooks include recipes, but Lizzie's unique cookbook

Cook Book vs. Cookbook

Throughout *A Recipe for Success,* you may notice that both the words cook book and cookbook are used. When Lizzie first started her cooking classes, books containing recipes were called cook books, but the words gradually became one word. This has happened with many other words in the English language, such as today and alright.

also offers advice on feeding a family, instructions for setting a table, and tips for removing stains. Best of all, it has raised millions of dollars to help children who live in Wisconsin's largest city, Milwaukee.

Lizzie did not plan on writing the most successful **fund-raising** cookbook in history, *The Settlement Cook Book*. She couldn't have imagined that the recipes used in her cooking classes would put good food on millions of tables around the world for more than 100 years. Perhaps your parents or your grandparents even have Lizzie's book in their kitchen. Why did Lizzie write it?

In 1901, Lizzie taught cooking to high school-age girls. The **immigrant** Jewish girls had recently moved to Milwaukee from countries in Eastern Europe like Russia or Poland. Everything in America was strange to them, including American foods. "I was trying to teach a group of young foreign girls in a crowded neighborhood how to cook simple and **nutritious** (noo **trish** uhss) food, yet have it attractive and inexpensive, as we prepare it in America," Lizzie said.

fund-raising: collecting money for a specific cause **immigrant:** someone who leaves a country to permanently live in another country **nutritious:** food containing substances that your body can use to help you stay strong and healthy

Eastern Europe and Russia

Jewish people came to the United States from countries in eastern Europe, such as Poland and Russia.

During the day, the girls went to school or worked at a job. Late in the afternoon, they attended Lizzie's cooking classes. For their own safety, they needed to return to their homes before dark because city streets could be dangerous, even back then. Because copy machines and computers hadn't been invented yet, the girls spent a lot of their time just writing down Lizzie's recipes from the chalkboard. Lizzie came up with the idea to publish a cookbook of her recipes so the girls would not waste their time copying them. Then they could safely get home.

This book tells the story of Lizzie, the cookbook she created, and how she helped immigrant Jewish families in Milwaukee. Most of the people Lizzie helped were poor. They had moved to America to make a better life for their families. Just like immigrants today, they arrived in America needing help with many new things: learning English, getting to know about the clothes we wear, the foods we eat, and the laws of our country. For more than 60 years, Lizzie helped new families in many different ways.

Lizzie's main goal was to make life better for the people in her community. During her lifetime, Lizzie was an author, a teacher, a newspaper columnist, a **truant officer**, a school board member, and the president of a community center. She

truant officer: someone who finds children who do not show up for school

helped to create Milwaukee's first **nursery** school and public playground. But she is most famous for her cookbook, which has sold more than 2 million copies and is still raising money to help children in Milwaukee today. Why did Lizzie devote her life to helping other people, especially those who were poor? Her story begins in 1858, shortly before the beginning of the American Civil War.

nursery: a place where babies and very young children are looked after while their parents are at work

1

The Teachers Kissed Us Good-bye

Which are the cleverest bees?
Spelling bees.
What sound do porcupines make when they kiss?
Ouch!

In 1844, Lizzie's parents, John and Mary Black, moved to Milwaukee from a small farm in Green Bay, Wisconsin. Many years later, John told his children stories about living on this farm in a clearing surrounded by woods. He told them about trading with Indians, and how the wolves howled at night outside the cabin door. Perhaps farming life was too difficult or the wolves were too scary, or maybe they

John Black

Mary Pereles Black

simply wanted to live closer to Mary's family. Whatever the reason, the Blacks decided to move to Milwaukee. They lived above the family business, a **dry goods store.**

On May 28, 1858, the Blacks welcomed the birth of their fourth child, Elizabeth. Everyone called her Lizzie. She had an older brother and 2 older sisters. Before long, she'd have a younger sister and brother, too. The 6 children played happily together in a home filled with dancing, music, games, and mischief. The sisters sometimes had pillow fights until their father called out from the next room, "Less noise, girls, less noise," and then they knew it was time to go to bed. In winter, they sledded down small hills and ice-skated on the Milwaukee River.

These ice skaters from the late nineteenth century are enjoying the same wintertime activity that people do today.

Although in most families only the boys went to school, when Lizzie was 4 years old, she became one of the

dry goods store: general store that sold a variety of items like dry foods such as sugar and flour and cloth

2

first girls to attend the Fifth Ward School. For the first day of school, Lizzie wrote that she was "dressed in her best **bib and tucker**, her hair carefully curled and tied up with a pretty pink ribbon, her face washed until it fairly shone." Together with her older brother and sister, Lizzie walked to the Fifth Ward School a few blocks from her home on the south side of Milwaukee.

This photo from about 1869 shows 2 children wearing clothes similar to the ones Lizzie would have worn.

What was Lizzie's school like? She remembered that her classroom had "a big pail of drinking water on a chair in the back part of the room and whenever

any pupil was thirsty, she got up and helped herself to a drink from the dipper that was in the pail. And, we had the dearest, sweetest teachers, who always kissed us good bye when we went home."

Lizzie and other students used a dipper to drink water from a pail.

bib and tucker: best clothes

"There were the spelling bees." These, she wrote, were "real social affairs, all of the classes in all of the schools indulged in them, with fond parents and friends near by to watch and encourage. Then at times the best spellers from each school were selected and we had a grand competitive spelling bee. The last 3 ones to be spelled down got cash prizes from **Prominent** Citizens."

To learn the multiplication tables, Lizzie's sister Julia said they sang a "catchy, childish melody. This jingle became one of our favorite songs, and served its purpose, for we mastered multiplication."

Lizzie remembered teachers punishing "bad" children by making them wear a cone-shaped paper cap called a **dunce cap**. In Lizzie's school, "any one that was backward or lazy had to don that cap and stand in full view of the school for the day. Sometimes these dunces would take it very seriously—and weep bitter tears

This student has to wear a dunce cap because he misbehaved.

prominent: famous or important
dunce cap: cone-shaped paper cap that misbehaving students were forced to wear in the classroom as punishment

of humiliation and again others when the teacher's back was turned would play all kinds of tricks to make the rest of the pupils laugh."

At the end of eighth grade, students had to pass a test in all of the subjects they'd studied to be able to graduate and attend East Side High School, the only high school in Milwaukee. Students traveled from all over the city to attend the high school. Lizzie wrote that the 112 students "came from all manners of houses,

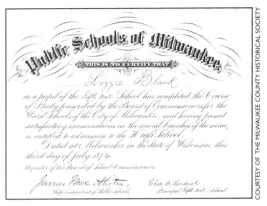

Lizzie's graduation certificate from the Fifth Ward School

East Side High School

our ages ranging from 12–20. Some of us were tall and some were short. Some were **stout** and some were lean. Some were wise and some otherwise, but all were proud...."

stout: quite fat; large and heavily built

5

A Really Difficult Exam

During the 1870s, students in Milwaukee had to pass an examination in order to advance to high school. Lizzie passed her exam in 1875. Although there is no existing record of that particular exam, the Milwaukee exam from 1878 still exists. It is likely that this exam was similar to the one Lizzie had passed 3 years earlier. Twenty out of the 139 students who took this exam failed it. How well would you have done?

Sample Questions from the 1878 Milwaukee Schools Eighth Grade Examination

GRAMMAR

1. Write a sentence containing 2 uses of the apostrophe.

2. Define the parts into which grammar is divided.

3. Define the properties of nouns.

4. Write a composition of not less than 12 lines on one of the following subjects: Chas. Sumner, The Soldiers' Home, Books, Mountains, The Story of a Tree, Wisconsin.

READING

1. Define articulation and accent.

2. Give 2 rules for the falling inflection.

3. Give the number of elementary sounds in each of the following words: brought, appoint, session, respond, and laugh.

ARITHMETIC

1. From one billion, ten thousand, one hundred and six thousandths, take 999,990,905,00505.

2. (a) Define number and integer.
   (b) Find the greatest common divisor of 12, 18, 21, and 36.

3. If 52 men can dig a trench 355 feet long, 60 feet wide, and 8 feet deep in 15 days, how long will a trench be that is 45 feet wide and 10 feet deep, which 45 men can dig in 25 days?

4. A, B, and C bought a farm in partnership. A paid ¼ of the purchase money, B ⅓, and C the rest. They sold it at a gain of $3,000. What was each one's share of the gain?

PENMANSHIP

Write the following stanza 3 times:

Sweet hour! that bids the laborer cease;
That gives the weary team release,
And leads them home, and crowns them there
With rest and shelter, food and care.

UNITED STATES HISTORY

1. Give an account of the voyage made by Francis Drake in 1579.

2. In the colony of Massachusetts, what persons were privileged to vote?

3. When and where did the first colonial Congress meet? What was done by this Congress?

4. Explain the following terms: "Right of Search," "Orders in Council," "Milan Decree," "Embargo Act," and "Monroe Doctrine."

GEOGRAPHY

1. Define cascades, gorges, equator, horizon, and glaciers.

2. Name the river systems of South America.
   (a) Territory drained by each.
   (b) Three principal rivers of each.

3. Give the form of government, the prevailing religion, the principal occupations, and the capital city of each of the following countries: Germany, France, Italy, Denmark, and England.

4. Draw a map of Wisconsin, and locate upon it the largest river, the largest lake, and the 7 largest cities.

PHYSIOLOGY

1. Describe the following membranes and give the functions of each: serous, synovial, and mucus.

2. (a) Describe muscle.
   (b) What are voluntary muscles? What are involuntary? Give an example of each.

3. (a) Name the digestive organs.
   (b) Describe the pancreas.

4. Give the anatomy of the ear.

ALGEBRA

1. Define quantity, algebra, root, and exponent.

2. Find the value of x in the following equation:

$$\frac{7x + 9}{4} - \left(x - \frac{2x-1}{9}\right) = 7.$$

8. Given $\frac{x}{2} + \frac{y}{3} = 7$ and $\frac{x}{3} + \frac{y}{2} = 8$ to find x and y.

MUSIC

1. Give the signatures of the following minor scales:

   G minor; D minor; C minor; and B minor.

2. When 6 sharps are at the beginning of a piece of music, what is the name of the key?

3. Write the meaning of the following musical terms: andante, adagio, poco a poco, colla parte, vivo, vivace, rit, a tempo, ma non troppo, largo, allegro.

4. How do you beat 6–8 time?

Lizzie lived far from East Side High School, so she and her friends "bought our lunch at the nearest grocery—consisting in most instances of crackers, pickles, and popcorn…." What would your parents say if you had crackers and pickles and popcorn for lunch?

Lizzie admired her teachers. She particularly liked the interesting activities assigned by her biology teacher, Professor Peckham. Professor Peckham taught students about parts of the body—both animal and human bodies. "He had us pick up all kinds of bones we could find in the streets and compare them with the **corresponding** bones of man. At one time when he **dissected** a cat in view of the whole class, many of the girls fainted…."

After school was over each day, Lizzie worked in her family's store. She helped customers and kept a record of the store's sales. Although girls rarely worked as salespeople during the 1870s, Lizzie's parents felt it was important not to hide their daughter from her neighborhood and the world around her.

corresponding: matching or going along with in some way **dissected:** cut open for study

10

Lizzie was known for her bravery. When she was a little girl, she met General Ulysses S. Grant, who later became the president of the United States. He held out his arms to greet Lizzie and her older sister Julia at a party held in his honor.

Julia hid with fright, but Lizzie went right up to the general to tug on his coat buttons and happily receive a kiss. The story of that kiss traveled around the entire neighborhood.

Ulysses S. Grant

Lizzie grew up during a difficult time in the United States. In 1861, when Lizzie was 3 years old, Abraham Lincoln became the sixteenth president of the United States. Soon after his election, the Civil War began and lasted until April 14, 1865. The Civil War was fought between Northern and Southern states. Among other things, the North and South disagreed over the question of slavery. The South supported slavery; the North

Abraham Lincoln

opposed it. The North won. Many American men on both sides died, and feelings between the 2 regions remained tense for many years.

Only 5 days after the war ended on April 14, 1865, John Wilkes Booth, a bitter man who had supported the South, **assassinated** (uh **sass** uh nay ted) President Lincoln. Lizzie's father, John, hated violence. Julia wrote that the only time she saw her father cry was when President Lincoln was killed.

The Black family was Jewish, and many of their beliefs came from their religion. Lizzie's parents taught their children that they had a responsibility to help the poor and to work to make the world a better place to live. They also believed that girls should learn how to be good homemakers—to cook, to clean, and to raise a family. According to Lizzie's mother, Mary, a woman's most important job was to provide her family with a happy and healthy home. She trained her daughters for marriage and homemaking, not to work outside the home.

assassinated: killed, usually someone who is well-known

The Blacks were middle-class; Lizzie's father earned enough money to support the family. In the late 1800s, middle-class women did not work for **wages**. Only women who needed to work to support their families got jobs outside the home. Lizzie followed her parents' wishes. She married, became a successful homemaker, and worked to help other people throughout her lifetime.

wages: the money someone is paid for his or her work

2

When I'm President

Who was the president after the first president of the United States? The second president.

Lizzie's 1877 report card from Milwaukee's East Side High School

What would you do if you were the president of the United States? Would you work for world peace? Would you give kids the right to vote? Would you pass a law to make recess last 6 hours every day?

In 1878, Lizzie graduated from East Side High School. She had excellent grades, and her classmates liked and admired her. They elected her the **valedictorian** (val uh dik **tor** ee uhn) of the graduating class. As the valedictorian, Lizzie spoke at the graduation

valedictorian: the student, usually with the highest grades in the class, who speaks at graduation

14

ceremonies on the topic "When I'm President." The title must have told her audience that Lizzie had a sense of humor. In 1878, women could not even vote, much less run for elected office. They would not gain that right for another 42 years. Yet Lizzie must have known about famous women like Susan B.

Anthony and Elizabeth Cady Stanton. They believed that women deserved the right to vote and to be treated as equals.

Susan B. Anthony

Elizabeth Cady Stanton

What did Lizzie say in her speech? First, she spoke about justice. She complained that the "wealth of the nation is in the hands of a few individuals … while the poor are becoming more miserable." To fix the problems of the nation, she challenged politicians to return to the simple values of "truth, honesty, virtue, and love." Who could solve this crisis? Women, argued Lizzie. Since women knew how to run their own homes successfully, they also knew how to govern the larger "home" of their city. If women applied their skills as mothers and homemakers to the problems of government, they could make the nation healthy again.

The Battle for Women's Right to Vote

In 1872, Victoria Woodhull became the first woman candidate for president of the United States. It was illegal for women to vote in the United States back then, but Victoria found out that no laws kept them from holding public office. She lost the election, but the winner, President Ulysses S. Grant, reportedly told her she might occupy his office someday.

Victoria Woodhull

COURTESY CHICAGO HISTORICAL SOCIETY

Susan B. Anthony voted in that same presidential election on November 5 in Rochester, New York. A few weeks later, she was arrested and eventually fined $100 for breaking the law against women voting. The trial judge opposed woman **suffrage (suf ridj)** and wrote his decision even before the trial had started.

The fight for women's right to vote was organized in the mid-nineteenth century. The people who campaigned for this right were called suffragists. (They were also sometimes called suffragettes.) Suffragists fought not only for the right to vote but also against other terrible inequalities in the law. For example, it was unlawful for a woman to sue for damages. In 1873, a woman

suffrage: the right to vote in an election

in Massachusetts slipped on the ice and injured herself. She could not sue, but her husband was awarded $1,300 for *his* loss of her ability to work. Leaders of the suffrage movement believed that if women had the vote, they would use it to gain other rights, too.

Many people believe the suffrage movement first began in 1848 in Seneca Falls, New York. Two leading suffragists, Lucretia Mott and Elizabeth Cady Stanton, called a women's rights convention in Seneca Falls where Stanton lived. Two hundred women and 40 men met and passed a **resolution** (rez uh **loo** shun) calling for women's right to vote. The woman suffrage movement in the United States would fight this battle for the next 72 years.

Lucretia Mott

LIBRARY OF CONGRESS, PRINTS AND PHOTOGRAPHS DIVISION LC-USZ62-42559 DLC

Women finally won the right to vote in 1920, when Congress adopted the Nineteenth Amendment to the U.S. Constitution. In 1919, Wisconsin was the first state to support the Nineteenth Amendment. The passage of woman suffrage had the immediate result of granting 26 million women, half the nation's population, the right to vote.

resolution: a course of action decided on by a meeting; agreed to by a vote

In her valedictorian speech, Lizzie also joked about eliminating high schools. "I have spent a good deal of my time considering the question of High Schools, and I came to the conclusion that the best thing I can do, is to abolish every one in the land." Why? So that girls can spend their days reading novels. Boys? Their time would be better spent chopping wood and "waiting patiently to hear the result of the last game of baseball." Without high schools, kids wouldn't become grown-ups who "bore people to death" with the useless information they usually learn in high school, Lizzie joked.

Lizzie ended her speech by reminding her audience that they'd be wise to place her name on the ticket as one of the candidates for the presidency in the next election. Lizzie's speech was greeted with long, loud applause. She received several baskets and bouquets of flowers. Her speech was so good that the *Milwaukee News*, a local newspaper, printed the entire speech the next day. A reporter called it "the event of the evening ... certainly the best **satire** (**sat** ire) on American politics I have listened to or read."

satire: humorous criticism

Although Lizzie never became the president of the United States, 22 years later, she would become the president of the Settlement House, an organization that helped thousands of men, women, and children. She was carrying out ideas that she had stated in her speech as class valedictorian. In her way, she was helping make life better for the larger "home" of her city, Milwaukee.

3

The Matchbox Boy

What did the frog say when she made a mistake while sewing?
Ripp-itt! Ripp-itt!
How did the tailor feel at the end of the day?
Sew sew.
How do you get an elephant into a matchbox?
Take all of the matches out first.

When Lizzie graduated from high school, she had to decide what she wanted to do next in her life, just as kids today have to make the same decision. Lizzie's family had enough money so that she did not need to work to help support her family, as girls often did in the late 1800s. Girls rarely went to college, and most of the girls who graduated from high school with Lizzie soon married and became housewives and mothers. Although Lizzie did not need to find a paying job, her family expected that until she married she would help people by volunteering.

Winter arrived early in 1878, and fierce snowstorms attacked Milwaukee. The newspapers were filled with stories about freezing temperatures in the **tenements** (**ten** uh munts) and the lack of warm winter clothing among the **needy**. Many of these poor people were Jewish immigrants—mostly Jews who had recently come from Russia and Poland. More and more of them arrived in Milwaukee lacking food, housing, clothes, and jobs.

WHI IMAGE ID 38114

Lizzie as a young woman, around 1880

These immigrants came to Milwaukee because they had been **persecuted** (pur suh **kyoo** tud) for their religious beliefs in their home countries. They had to leave their homes in order to survive and to

tenement: home for the poor, often in run-down condition   **needy:** very poor
persecuted: treated cruelly and unfairly because of religion or beliefs

make better lives for themselves and their families. They arrived exhausted from weeks of traveling across the ocean and halfway across the United States. Many traveled by steamboat from the Erie Canal across the Great Lakes. Few spoke English; most were uneducated, they wore different clothes, ate different foods, and often had no money. Unlike today, no government **agencies** (**ay** jen sees) existed in 1878 to help new immigrants settle in the United States. Sometimes private organizations and individuals helped them.

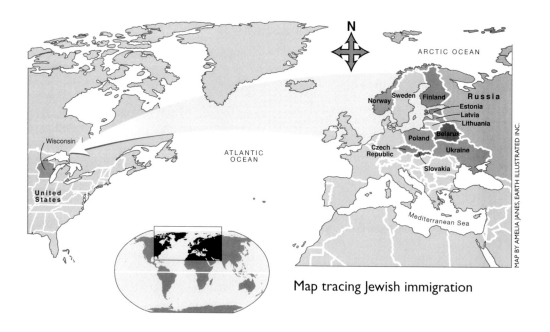

Map tracing Jewish immigration

agency: office or business that provides service to the public

This is where Lizzie comes in. After high school, Lizzie wanted to find work that was meaningful—work that helped other people. She saw the difficult challenges facing the poor Jewish families who had just come to America. She wanted to help each one to "learn our language, our laws, our customs, in order to obtain **suitable** work and become an honorable self-respecting citizen." She wanted to teach them to be successful in America.

How would you feel if your cousins from another country moved into your neighborhood? What would you think if you'd never met them before and they wore different clothes, spoke a different language, and behaved differently from you? Would you welcome them and help them to fit in? Would they embarrass you when you were with your friends? You may find both things true at the same time. You would want to help them fit in, but you might also feel embarrassed by their differences.

Lizzie wanted to help the new Jewish immigrants in Milwaukee because she hated what **poverty** (**pov** ur tee) did to people. She also had another reason for helping them.

suitable: right for a particular purpose   **poverty:** being poor

Lizzie's family had left Germany to come to the United States in the early 1840s. By the time Lizzie was born, her parents spoke English, wore American clothes, and had enough money to buy a house, food, and other things necessary for their children to live comfortably. Although they arrived as immigrants, they had become Americans.

The Russian immigrants of the 1880s were poorer than the earlier immigrants from Germany like Lizzie's parents. The Russian Jews embarrassed Lizzie and many of the other German Jews. The German Jews were afraid that the ways in which new immigrants looked and acted and even their poverty would lead to a rise of **anti-Semitism** (an tee **sem** ih tiz uhm), or negative feelings against *all* Jews. Lizzie wanted these new immigrants to fit in with other Americans and not stand out in a crowd. Lizzie said, "It is a selfish motive that spurs us on; it is to protect ourselves, our own reputation in the community that we must work with **tact**, with heart and soul to better the home conditions of our people."

anti-Semitism: hatred of and discrimination against Jews
tact: being sensitive to people and not upsetting or hurting anyone's feelings

In later years, Lizzie told a story that shows the mixture of concern and embarrassment she felt toward the immigrants. She said she was shopping in a furniture store and saw a boy of about 12 years old. He had a bright but rather dirty face and was selling matches. At that time, many young poor children sold matches because everybody needed them in their homes to light lamps and coal and wood stoves. The boy approached the owner of the store and offered his matches for sale "cheap." To Lizzie's embarrassment, the "matchbox boy" had "attracted the attention of everyone within hearing!" Lizzie followed the boy out of the store and asked him why he wasn't in school. He said he needed to work to help support his family. Lizzie felt sad that the boy couldn't go to school because his family was so poor. But she also worried that other people would somehow think less of the German Jewish community after seeing this little Jewish peddler.

Lizzie was educated, full of energy, and worked hard to make the world a better place to live, especially for people who lived in poverty. As soon as she graduated from high school, Lizzie volunteered to work for the Ladies Relief Sewing Society.

In Milwaukee, as in other American cities, women like Lizzie who did not have to work *chose* to make themselves useful citizens. Similar women's groups were organized across the country. Lizzie was one of 50 women who promised to provide warm clothing for poor children. They sewed new clothes, repaired donated clothes, and gave families food, blankets, and sheets. Lizzie would get up by 5 a.m., finish her household chores, and spend the rest of the day doing volunteer work. She described her work as having to clothe "a lot of dirty, poor children and their mothers." So began Lizzie's lifelong **commitment** to helping the poor.

commitment: promise to do something or support something

4

A Penny for a Hot Bath

What do you call a fairy that hasn't taken a bath?
Stinkerbell.

Soon after finishing high school, Lizzie met Simon Kander, a traveling clothes salesman. They met through their shared interest in improving the public schools. Lizzie liked Simon as much as she liked volunteering for the Ladies Relief Sewing Society. They married on May 17, 1881, when Lizzie was 23 years old. Lizzie's engagement announcement described her as "one of the prettiest and most accomplished young ladies in town."

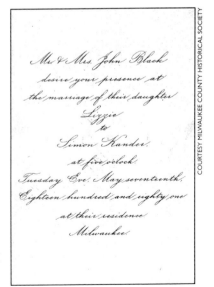

Invitation to Simon and Lizzie's wedding

Lizzie and Simon's marriage certificate

Lizzie and Simon, around 1880

Like Lizzie, Simon had a deep commitment to helping others. He started his own real estate business and was so successful that he was able to retire at a young age. He then volunteered for the Wisconsin Association for the Blind, served in the Wisconsin State Legislature, and served on the Milwaukee Board of School Directors (today called the Milwaukee School Board). He was also a member and president of "The Old Settlers' Club," a group of "jolly good fellows" who met to remember and preserve Milwaukee's history.

Lizzie respected Simon's opinions and always asked his advice before joining an organization. They never had children of their own, but the *Milwaukee Sentinel* described Lizzie as having "a heart big enough to mother every child." Perhaps because Lizzie and Simon had no children of their own, they spent their time helping other families in their community.

After Lizzie had been married for 9 years, she became a truant officer for the South Side School Alliance. She began visiting the homes of Milwaukee's immigrant families to find out why their children were not attending school. The small, dirty apartments in which the children lived upset Lizzie. Even though the law said that girls must remain in school until the age of 14, many families sent girls as young as 10 years old to work because they needed the money. Other families did not send their children to school because the children lacked warm clothing.

Lizzie wanted the children to go to school. She convinced the South Side School Alliance to give the children warm clothing. Although she stopped working as a truant officer after 4 years, Lizzie never stopped caring about the children she had come to know. In 1895, when she was president of the Ladies Relief Sewing Society, Lizzie gave $75 of her own money to form the "Keep Clean Mission." The goal of the Mission was "to see that the children of our poor be kept clean and sent to school regularly." If the children attended school, Lizzie thought, they might learn and adopt American habits and values.

Trillions of Tiny Creatures

Why did the germ cross the microscope?
To get to the other slide.

Did you know that right now you are surrounded by trillions of tiny creatures? They're in your mouth, on your skin, and all over your body. Some of them are harmless, some are even helpful, but others can make you sick. Today, they are famous as "germs," but they weren't always well-known.

In the nineteenth century, many Americans lived with a great fear of the unknown. They were afraid of mysterious fevers and diseases that came and left unpredictably. These fears slowly began to disappear when scientists such as the French chemist Louis Pasteur (Pas **tchur**) discovered that animal and human diseases were often caused by tiny life forms called germs. The discovery of these "invisible enemies" caused a revolution in the households of America.

As people began to understand that germs cause diseases, they also realized that they could do something to prevent their spread. They could fight germs by keeping their homes clean, by cooking food at high temperatures for long periods of time, and by trying to avoid germs altogether.

31

Dust became an important target. By attacking the germs in dust, people could prevent the diseases caused by those germs. After cleaning their houses, homemakers would wait several hours for the dust to settle before preparing meals. That way, the dust in the air wouldn't land on the food they were cooking. Refrigerator surfaces had to be kept spotlessly clean to prevent germs from **contaminating** the food stored within. Cooks had to keep themselves clean by using aprons to protect food from their germ-filled clothes and by washing their hands often with **disinfectant** (dis in **fek** tunt) soap.

This "war against germs" continued outside the kitchen, too. Once-popular thick carpets that hid dust were replaced with wood floors and small area rugs. Daily bathing, once considered unsafe, was now encouraged as a healthy way to destroy germs. Men often shaved off the beards and moustaches that had been popular since the 1850s to prevent germs from finding a home in their facial hair. Kissing babies on the lips was discouraged, since germs could easily be passed this way. To prevent germs from spreading, women were encouraged to wear washable gloves when shopping.

Now, in the twenty-first century, we have the same concerns about germs. When you're asked to wash your hands before eating, feel proud that you're part of a tradition that's continued for more than 100 years. Or don't feel proud—but wash your hands anyway.

contaminating: making unclean   **disinfectant:** a substance that destroys germs

Lizzie and the other Keep Clean Mission women also wanted the children to develop skills to get good jobs. With good jobs, these young people could escape the boredom of working in factories. If children learned how to work with their hands, they could experience their own talents and creativity. The women hoped that children would also develop their love for beauty, order, and cleanliness. Such positive feelings and experiences would make them better people.

To attract children to the Mission, the women provided many board games to play, such as Parcheesi and checkers— games that these poor children couldn't afford to have at home. This plan failed. The children did not want to *play* games; they wanted to learn how to *do* things. "We might still be playing and preaching," Lizzie confessed many years later, "if some of the youngsters hadn't insisted on *doing* something."

Parcheesi: A Game That Began with Slaves as Pawns

Can you imagine playing a board game in which you could move real people as the pieces on the board? Parcheesi is a game thought to have been created in India around 500 BC. It was known then as *Pachisi, The Royal Game of India,* because emperors often played the game. The game "board" would be marked out on the grounds of their palace courtyards. The emperors would play *Pachisi* while sitting up on a 4-foot high platform. They'd direct the movements of 16 girl slaves, who were the **pawns** in the game. The girls would be dressed in red, yellow, blue, or green, the traditional

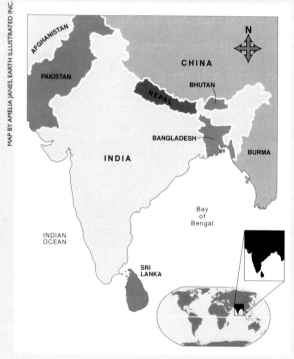

Parcheesi originated in India.

pawn: person or thing used to get something or gain an advantage

4 colors of Parcheesi game pieces. In the United States, people began playing Parcheesi as a board game in the 1850s.

The object of the game is take each of your 4 colored pawns from Start to your Home Base, which is located in the center square of the board. Rolls of the dice determine your moves. It sounds easy, but you can't even move out of Start until you roll a 5. Once you can move, you must avoid running into blockades and dodge your opponents, who threaten at every turn to send you back to Start. If you plan your moves wisely and use the safety zones scattered around the board, you just might win!

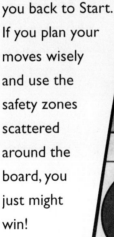

Parcheesi board

The name "Keep Clean Mission" became a problem. The immigrants did not like the idea that someone thought they needed outsiders to keep them clean. So, in 1896, the Keep Clean Mission's name was changed to the "Milwaukee Jewish Mission." The newly named mission offered classes in sewing, **crocheting** (kro **shay** ing), **embroidering** (em **broy** dur ing), making paper flowers, jack-knife work (woodcarving), and

WHI IMAGE ID 7023

Joseph Schlitz Brewing Company

painting. One hundred children eagerly attended the classes, anxious for every opportunity to learn. As she **demonstrated** throughout her life, Lizzie could change her plans to respond to the needs and desires of the community she served.

Lizzie still wanted the immigrants to stay clean. Along with the Mission women, she established

crocheting: using a special hooked needle to make a kind of needlework from thread or yarn
embroidering: sewing a picture or design onto cloth   **demonstrated:** showed something by doing it

a public bathhouse, since many families had no place for bathing in their own homes. The Mission was located next to the Schlitz beer brewing plant. To create the bathhouse, the brewery piped in the extra hot water it used to wash beer bottles. Children were given lectures on cleanliness, and their families could bathe in the bathhouses. For a penny, a person could enjoy a hot bath. Would you pay a penny, a nickel, or even a dollar for a hot bath or shower if that were the only way you could bathe?

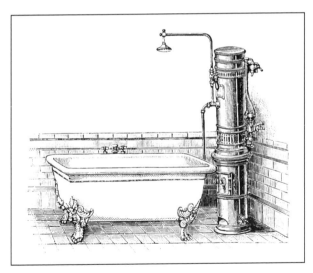

5

Did You Wash Your Hands?

What's the worst thing about being an octopus?
Washing your hands before dinner.
A man walks into a doctor's office. He has a cucumber up his nose,
a carrot in his left ear, and a banana in his right ear.
"What's the matter with me?" he asks the doctor.
The doctor replies, "You're not eating properly."

What skills were important for girls in the late 1800s? Sewing and cooking were 2 important skills. If girls could sew, they could make their own clothing and might be able to find work as a seamstress. There weren't too many good jobs for young women at that time. But women who could sew were able to work in the growing **garment** industry.

Women learning to cook a nutritious meal on a low budget could help their families to stay healthy. Lizzie believed that

garment: item of clothing

women had an important role in the family: to keep a **thrifty**, clean, and healthy household. She thought this would keep families safe from poverty and set them on the road to success.

The Mission's sewing school met every day after school for 1½ hours. Girls ages 7 to 14 attended. The teachers taught the girls how to sew, make dresses, and draw a dress pattern. The Mission expected that in learning to sew, the girls would also learn neatness, carefulness, and patience.

By 1898, the Mission had begun offering cooking classes for girls from ages 13 to 15. Lizzie and other volunteers taught girls how to cook, bake, and build a fire for the cooking stove. People did not have electric or gas stoves, and microwaves were nearly 100 years in the future! Each girl would prepare her own dish, often with her mother, older sisters, or friends watching. Though the immigrant girls may have been skilled in cooking the meals from their own countries, Lizzie thought that this was not enough. The cooking classes taught the immigrant girls how to buy and prepare American foods.

thrifty: careful with money

Lizzie also taught that the way the food looked when it was served was just as important as the nutritional value of the food. In other words, food must look good as well as be good for you. The Mission attempted to teach proper ways to set the table and prepare clean, healthy meals. Of course, cleanliness mattered in the kitchen, too! The most commonly heard phrase in the school was, "Did you wash your hands?"

More and more girls attended the classes after school or work and were learning important skills. But as the cooking classes and other Mission programs became more popular, Lizzie felt frustrated by the lack of space that limited the number of activities the Mission could offer. She needed more space and she needed more money to keep the Mission operating.

Lizzie began to raise money so that the Mission could move to a larger building. She contacted several business friends of her husband, Simon. She convinced them to give money to the Mission. *The Sentinel*, a local newspaper, complimented Lizzie for her fund-raising achievements. The reporter wrote that Lizzie was successful because of the men and women who believe "that the only solution of the problem of the poor lies in the education of the children." When Lizzie had raised enough **pledges** for a yearly income

of $1,000, the Mission rented a pleasant home at 507 Fifth Street between Cherry and Galena Streets in downtown Milwaukee. In May 1900, the Mission combined with

COURTESY OF MILWAUKEE JEWISH HISTORICAL SOCIETY

The old Settlement House on Fifth Street

another Jewish charity, the Sisterhood of Personal Service, which had started a night school for immigrants, to form "The Settlement."

pledge: promise to donate money

The "Jane Addams of Milwaukee"

Lizzie Kander often was called the "Jane Addams of Milwaukee." What did this mean, and who was Jane Addams?

Jane Addams

Jane Addams was born in 1860. She grew up in the village of Cedarville, Illinois. When she was 6 years old, she went with her father to the nearby city of Freeport. She saw houses that were falling down and children wearing torn, dirty shirts playing in the mud. Jane realized that these people must be very poor. As she left town with her father, Jane told him, "Daddy, when I grow up, I am going to buy a nice big house. Then I shall invite all the poor children to play in my yard and house whenever they want." Twenty-three years later, she did just that.

In 1889, Jane began looking for a big house in the middle of a poor neighborhood where many immigrants lived. She found just the right house on Chicago's West Side. A wealthy man named Charles Hull had built the 2-story, red brick house 33 years earlier. When Jane explained to the owner of the house at the time, Helen Culver, that she wanted to use the house to help poor people in the neighborhood, Helen said that her cousin Charles would have liked Jane's plan. She let Jane rent it for only one dollar a year. Jane was so grateful that she named the building Hull House.

Hull House was one of the first settlement houses in the United States. Its goal was to help poor people help themselves. The settlement provided services for the families in the neighborhood, including a kindergarten and day-care facilities for children of working mothers, a night school for adults, a place for club meetings for older children, an art gallery, and libraries. Jane's friend Ellen Starr offered lessons in cooking and sewing for young girls. Hungry children learned that they could visit the house and buy milk and spaghetti for a penny. On cold winter nights, adult workers found that Hull House provided bowls of soup for a nickel or a dime. Inspired by Hull House, settlement houses—including the ones in Milwaukee—began to form throughout the United States. They offered many of the same services that Hull House provided.

Jane Addams lived and worked in Hull House until her death in 1935. She became one of the most influential women in the country through her settlement work, her writing, and her efforts for world peace. In 1931, she received the Nobel Peace Prize. Each year this prize is given to the person who has done more than anyone else in the world to help people live together in peace. When Lizzie was called the "Jane Addams of Milwaukee," it was because she, too, was responsible for helping poor immigrants to lead better lives. She couldn't have been paid a higher compliment.

6

President Lizzie

Why did the man have lunch at the bank?
Because he wanted to eat rich food.

The Milwaukee Settlement House became known
as simply the Settlement. It was one of more than 400
settlements scattered throughout the United States by 1910.
The settlements hoped to teach immigrants, and especially
their children, how to become good Americans. Sometimes
the wealthier people who helped run settlements actually
"settled"—that is, they chose to live—near the settlement
houses. Living in the neighborhood, they got to know the
people they served as neighbors. The settlement workers
were no longer visitors from "better" parts of town.

Lizzie was chosen to be the Milwaukee Settlement's
first president, a position she would hold for the next 18

Jewish immigrant district

years. The Settlement was located in the heart of the Jewish immigrant district. This made it easy for the immigrant children and their families to participate in Settlement House activities. The building also was selected because it was located next to the Jung Brewery, which provided hot water for the Settlement bathhouse.

When it opened, the Settlement immediately exploded with activity. It drew in as many as 1,300 visitors each week. The baths were the Settlement's most popular service. The immigrants particularly welcomed the baths because many lived in overcrowded houses with no indoor toilets or baths. According to Settlement records, 17,000 baths were taken during the first year and 23,582 baths were taken during 1906.

The baths had 2 purposes. They satisfied the desire of Lizzie and her co-workers to help the immigrants appreciate the value of keeping clean. They also attracted people to the Settlement. Lizzie reported:"Many of their [students'] mothers as well as their older sisters and friends who come to the baths visit the classes and linger around, interested and eager **spectators**. Once lured into the wholesome surroundings of the Settlement with the lure of hot water, the older men and women took advantage of the many communal activities designed to teach them about the U.S."

The Settlement had classes and activities for all ages and interests: sewing, dressmaking, woodworking, dancing, a play area for babies and their mothers, and, of course, cooking classes, many of which Lizzie herself taught. It sponsored clubs with names like "Busy Bees," "Jolly Workers," "Good Sports," "Newsboys Literary Circle," and "Rosebud

spectator: someone who watches an event and does not participate in it

Club." Girls learned how to crochet slippers, weave small rugs and hammocks for dolls, and make **chatelaines** (sha tu **lens**). They were taught to sew and **darn** different types of canvas and then apply these lessons in hemming towels and making laundry bags and aprons. The boys of the Settlement learned carpentry and made useful household objects like cabinets. Debating clubs and whittling classes aimed to keep the boys off the streets and out of mischief.

Young and old joined the programs, which ran from 9 a.m. until 11 p.m. Children filled the classes in the afternoon. The night school offered classes in American history and English to help adults with citizenship skills. By 1906, the Settlement offered 13 levels of sewing classes, 5 classes in English, 2 dancing classes, 7 afternoon girls' clubs, one Saturday night **drilling** club, gymnastics instruction, and afternoon as well as evening parties. The Milwaukee Public Library even opened a branch in the reading room of the Settlement.

chatelaine: old fashioned chain worn at the waist by women for carrying keys or purses   **darn:** to repair clothing by sewing crossed stitches very close together   **drilling:** exercises designed to develop a skill, such as marching in complicated formations like bands do at football games

Lizzie saw each little girl as a future wife and mother. It bothered her that the children's mothers, often alone at home, could not participate in Settlement activities. Many of the mothers had become curious and wanted to learn more about how their daughters were learning to cook. To involve the mothers, Lizzie started a Mothers' Club. Its members included both

WHI IMAGE ID 38113

Lizzie wearing a fancy hat

wealthier volunteer women and poorer immigrant women. The Mothers' Club met on Wednesday afternoons. During meetings, volunteers presented short talks on **home economics**, child care, and other topics of importance to women. Afterwards, everyone chatted over cookies. Far ahead of her time, Lizzie turned the Settlement basement into a day-care center and provided adult supervision so that the mothers could attend the meetings.

home economics: science and art of managing a household

The Settlement played an important role in many families' lives. Ida Rapkin, whose family participated in many Settlement activities, explained, "You can't know what the Settlement meant to us. Our parents were immigrants. We 3 sisters learned—today we'd call it home economics—and played at parties celebrating Jewish and American holidays. And Papa proudly went to citizenship classes and learned English. So at the Settlement, immigrant families learned how to be good Americans."

Even though she was the president of the Settlement, Lizzie continued teaching cooking to the immigrant girls and women. She always searched for ways to improve the Settlement's services and activities. A seemingly small problem she solved in one of those cooking classes would change the kitchens of America forever.

7

You Are What You Eat

Why did the cook get arrested?
Because he beat up an egg.
Why do people become bakers?
Because they need the dough.

Think about food: the smells can make you hungry, the tastes can make you happy. Slice an onion, and it can make you cry. Eat too much pizza, and it can give you a  stomachache. Food plays an important part in our lives. When we gather for birthdays, holidays, and parties, we celebrate with food. If you can affect the way people think about food, you can **influence** their lives in an important way. Lizzie understood this, and her cooking classes and cookbook became her passport into the kitchens of millions of homemakers.

influence: to have an effect on someone or something

The Settlement's ability to survive depended upon Lizzie's ability to raise money to support it. Many of the early supporters were friends of her husband, Simon. For the Settlement House to continue to exist, it needed a more dependable source of funding. Lizzie found the solution to her financial problem by drawing upon one of the most popular activities of the Settlement, her own cooking classes.

Shortly after the Settlement opened, Lizzie found that the girls in her cooking classes wasted too much time in class writing down the simple recipes from a chalkboard. Copy machines hadn't been invented in 1901, and Lizzie felt the girls' time would be better spent actually cooking, instead of copying recipes. Since classes met after school and the high school-age girls had to be home before dark for safety reasons, it made sense to print the recipes so that the girls could practice their cooking at home.

During one meeting of the Settlement's Cooking Committee, Lizzie suggested publishing a cookbook. The cookbook could combine the lessons from her cooking classes with recipes contributed by her friends. Time spent

51

in copying recipes could be saved for practicing cooking, and seeing the recipes printed in a book might convince the immigrant parents to adopt American cooking habits. The committee gladly supported printing the recipes and cooking lessons.

Lizzie asked the men of the Settlement Board for $18 to pay for a booklet of recipes and household tips. It was a worthy project, they said, but they refused her request because the money had not been set aside in the year's budget. They jokingly added that they would gladly "share in any profits from your little **venture**."

Lizzie would not take "no" for an answer. She showed her collection of recipes to Merton Yewdale, the owner of a Milwaukee printing company. He asked to show it to his wife. Lizzie later said, "Well, she was just enthusiastic about them. So he suggested that we have them printed in book form, and even offered to help get sufficient funds through advertising to cover the printing and binding…. All our friends, who were outstanding housekeepers, rallied to the cause. With their help we added to this collection a number of more

venture: a project that is somewhat risky

elaborate recipes that for years were used and reused in the families." In addition to the favorite recipes of the committee members, families of the students contributed recipes of some of their favorite foreign dishes.

Mr. Yewdale assisted the Cooking Committee by finding businesses in Milwaukee to pay for advertisements in the cookbook. With help from this friendly printer, the first edition of 1,000 cookbooks was printed in 1901. Lizzie and the women of the Settlement hoped that any extra copies not needed by students could be sold for 50 cents to the general public.

The Settlement Cook Book: The Way to a Man's Heart was a hit from the start. All the copies were sold within the first year of printing. "Imagine how relieved we were when, in a little over a year, the entire edition was exhausted," Lizzie said in a radio interview many years later. How fortunate were the men of the Settlement Board, who had shown so little confidence in the project! The profits from the sale of future editions of the cookbook would allow the committee to build and own larger and larger community centers.

8

Cracker Gruel and Frogs Legs and Fried Mush, Oh My!

Why did the cookie go to the hospital?
Because he was feeling crummy.

Cookbooks tell stories. Every cookbook tells the tale of how food is created from a set of directions and ingredients. *The Settlement Cook Book* also told the story about how immigrants could fit into American culture. Lizzie believed that the young girls in her classes would become better Americans by buying food, cooking, and managing their kitchens the way she did. She believed that the lessons she learned from her mother were good examples of a well-run American household. She wanted to teach these girls and their mothers how to cook with foods and equipment very different from what they had known in their native countries—sometimes with foods and cooking tools they'd never seen before.

At the beginning of the twentieth century, an American cookbook was expected to contain not only recipes for the popular dishes of the day, but also everything from cures for leaking faucets to directions for washing dirty hands. A cookbook devoted entirely to food was unthinkable! And as more people believed that science could solve the problems of the world, cookbook authors began to apply scientific principles to cooking. Where older cookbooks had asked for a "handful of this" or "a pinch of that," recipes now called for exact "scientific" measures like "a level teaspoon" ("run the back of a knife along the bowl of the spoon, to level off the top").

Lizzie and her co-author, Mrs. Henry Schoenfeld, chairman of the Settlement Cooking School Committee, wrote *The Settlement Cook Book* during this period in which scientific knowledge guided household tasks such as cooking and cleaning. Their book provided lessons about "American food, proper nutrition, sanitation in cooking, and economy of food preparation, which was so important to them."

The subtitle of the book, *The Way to a Man's Heart,* also expressed the authors' belief in the power of food. Their goal was to help housewives create happy and healthy homes. What better way to make their men happy than by serving them delicious meals? The way to a man's heart *is* through his stomach, they believed. One look at Simon Kander would assure you that this was true for Lizzie's husband!

Lizzie and her husband, Simon, in their later years

The cookbook was 174 pages long, including the advertisements, and was divided into 2 sections. The first section, "The Recipes," contained 500 recipes for experienced cooks. Lizzie had acquired the recipes from the proud hands of her friends, many well-known for setting "some of the finest tables in Milwaukee." The second section, "Lessons in Cookery," contained simple recipes for beginning cooks. Lizzie had been testing these recipes for 20 years in her cooking classes.

The "Recipes" section introduced the young girls and their families to American dishes and ingredients and local favorites. The recipes were a mixture of German, Eastern European, American, and Jewish cooking. The book introduced the immigrant women to American foods, such as baking powder biscuits, pot roast, doughnuts, hasty pudding, celery salad, graham muffins, creamed cod, gingerbread, orange-banana custard, and Boston browned potatoes. It also included many traditional German dishes, such as **hasen pfeffer** (**hah** ssen feff ur), **pfeffernusse** (**feff** ur nooss), and **kuchen** (**kuk** ken). There were Jewish specialties as well, such as **kugel** (**koo** gull), **matzah** (**maht** zuh) **balls**, **gefilte** (guh **fel** tuh) **fish**, and other **kosher** (**koh** shur) recipes.

WHI IMAGE ID 38116

With Best Wishes
Mrs. Simon Kander.

hasen pfeffer: marinated rabbit   pfeffernusse: holiday cookie   kuchen: coffee cake
kugel: baked noodle pudding
matzah ball: dumpling-like ball made of matzah meal, eggs, and oil, boiled in chicken soup
gefilte fish: ground fish filled with seasoning, served cold
kosher: food prepared according to Jewish dietary laws

No Peanut Butter and Jelly?

What did the jelly say to the peanut butter?
Stick with me and we'll go places.

The third edition (1907) of *The Settlement Cook Book* featured a new "Sandwiches" section that included recipes for preparing "Swiss Cheese Sandwiches," "Jelly Sandwiches," "Lettuce Sandwiches," "Cottage Cheese Sandwiches," and "Peanut Paste [Butter] Sandwiches." In future editions, new sandwiches would be added including "Onion Sandwiches," "Horseradish Sandwiches," and "Cherry and Pineapple Sandwiches."

In the fourteenth edition (1925), the new "Menus" section offered suggestions for entire meals to serve for special events, ranging from "Afternoon Tea or Coffee" to "School Lunch Menus." The food for "Children's Birthday Menus" included "Animal Shaped Peanut and Jelly Sandwiches," with a reference to the 2 pages in the book containing the recipes for "Peanut Sandwiches" and "Jelly Sandwiches." None of the 23 editions of *The Settlement Cook Book* that Lizzie edited ever included a recipe combining peanut butter and jelly into one sandwich. Why? Because as far as historians are aware, no one had yet thought of combining peanut butter and jelly into one sandwich. Imagine!

No one really knows when or where the peanut butter and jelly sandwich was first created. What we do know is that soldiers in World War II were given **rations** (**rash** uns) of both peanut butter and jelly. It is said that the American soldiers added jelly to their peanut butter for variety and to make it taste better. Peanut butter didn't require refrigeration and provided an inexpensive and high-protein substitute to meat. It was an instant hit, and soldiers returning to the United States made peanut butter and jelly sales soar.

The "Lessons" section began by giving helpful household hints on everything from the correct way to remove crumbs between different parts of the meal ("Before the dessert is served, remove the crumbs from the cloth, either with a brush or a crumb knife.") to rules for waiting on the table ("Never fill glasses and cups more than three-quarters full...." "Serve the most honored guest first.") to directions for dusting a room ("Dust it from the highest things to the lowest.").

ration: food supply

The principles of scientific household management appeared throughout the cookbook. The "Food Classified" part in the "Lessons" section presented detailed information on the chemistry and nutritional values of foods ("It has often been claimed that an egg was equal to a pound of beef in nutrition. Such is not the case, though eggs stand high on the list.").

Charts listed the chemical ingredients of different foods such as bread and cereals.

Composition of Cereals

	Proteid	Fat	Starch	Mineral Matter	Water
Oatmeal	15.6	7.3	68.0	1.9	7.2
Cornmeal	8.9	2.2	75.1	.9	12.9
Entire Wheat Flour	14.2	1.9	70.6	1.2	12.1
Rice	7.8	.04	79.4	.4	12.4
Pearl Barley	9.3	1.0	77.6	1.3	19.8

99 LBS.NET WEIGHT

WHOLE BEAN UNCOATED

TABLE RICE

proteid: protein

The chapter on "Cereals and Fruits" began with the story of how food is digested.

Digestion of Foods

All food is changed into a liquid before it can be carried about by the blood, to build up the worn out tissues.

Digestion:

First step—In the mouth, the food is crushed and some of the starch is changed to sugar by the saliva.

Second step—In the stomach, the **gastric** juice dissolves the proteids (**pro** teeds).

Third step—Through the agency of the **bile, pancreatic** (**pan** kree at ik), and **intestinal** juices:

    a. The rest of the starch is changed to sugar

    b. The rest of the proteids are dissolved

    c. The fat is divided into small **globules**

gastric: to do with the stomach   bile: a green liquid that is made by the liver and helps digest food
pancreatic: having to do with the pancreas, a gland near the stomach that makes a fluid to help digest food
intestinal: having to do with the intestine, a long tube extending below the stomach that digests food and absorbs liquids and salts   globule: tiny ball, especially of liquid

The Settlement Cook Book contained directions for cooking with the newest kitchen gadgets. Recipes called for the use of the recently invented Dover egg beater, double boilers (2 saucepans, one fitting inside the other), angel food cake pans, ramekins (small fireproof dishes), and chafing dishes (a metal dish or pan placed above a heating device and used to either cook food or keep it warm at the table). Several merchants placed advertisements in the cookbook for gas stoves, which would replace old-fashioned wood-burning stoves.

Ramekin

Chafing Dish

Double Boiler

Dover Egg Beater

Angel Food Cake Pan

If you had a sweet tooth, *The Settlement Cook Book* was for you. In keeping with the fad of the times of baking with white flour and sugar, a fourth of the recipes were devoted to desserts. There were entire chapters on custards, puddings, pudding sauces, ice cream, sherbet, pastries, cakes, **tortes** (torts), cake frostings, and candies. You could find recipes for more than 20 different kinds of cookies, including plain, white, coconut, butter, chocolate, fruit, peanut, spice, and molasses cookies.

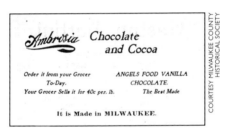

Along with recipes for desserts, the cookbook had ads for ingredients like cocoa and chocolate and for stores that sold sweets.

torte: cake in which ground nuts or crumbs are usually used instead of flour

Tales of Marshmallows

Why did the elephant stand on the marshmallow?
So she wouldn't fall in the hot chocolate.

Marshmallows are one of the earliest candies known to humankind. They were named marshmallows because the early recipe called for using sap from the root of the mallow plant, which grows wild in marshes. The first marshmallows were made by boiling pieces of the marsh-mallow root pulp with sugar until the mixture thickened. The mixture was then strained and cooled.

Campfire White Marshmallows ad

As early as 2000 BC, ancient Egyptians enjoyed the sweet now called the marshmallow. The gooey treat was combined with honey and considered so special that it was reserved for gods and royalty. Marshmallows became popular in the United States in the early 1900s after a new manufacturing process was developed in which candy makers replaced the mallow root with **gelatin**.

gelatin: a clear substance used in making jelly, desserts, and glue that is obtained from animal bones and tissue

Recipes for marshmallows first appeared in *The Settlement Cook Book* in the third edition (1907), with recipes for "Toasted or Roasted Marshmallows" and for "Marshmallow Fudge." The sixth edition (1913) added a recipe for "Marshmallow Frosting," and finally the seventh edition (1914) included a recipe for "Marshmallows," which explained how to make marshmallows from scratch. Marshmallows became so popular that the fifteenth edition (1926) even had a recipe for fake or "Mock Marshmallows," in which macaroons and egg whites were used to create an imitation marshmallow. The twenty-eighth edition (1947) of *The Settlement Cook Book* included recipes for "Caramel Covered Marshmallows," "Chocolate Marshmallow Icebox Dessert" (the ingredients are similar to s'mores), "Sweet Potatoes and Marshmallows," "Marshmallow Pudding," and "Marshmallow Sauce" to serve over ice cream. By the time the revised and updated *New Settlement Cookbook* appeared in 1991, the marshmallow fad had passed. The only marshmallow recipe remaining from earlier editions of *The Settlement Cook Book* was the recipe for making the marshmallows themselves.

Marshmallow Fudge

2 cups sugar   2 ounce squares of bitter chocolate

1 cup milk or cream   1 tablespoon butter

½ pound marshmallows

Heat sugar and milk, add chocolate, and boil until it hardens in cold water. Just before it is done add a small piece of butter, then begin to stir in marshmallows, crushing and beating them with a spoon. Continue to stir in marshmallows after the fudge has been taken from the fire, until half a pound has been stirred into the fudge. Cool in sheets ¾ of an inch thick and cut in cubes.

Sweet Potatoes and Marshmallows

12 sweet potatoes or 1 can of sweet potatoes

¼ cup fat   ½ teaspoon salt

¼ cup sugar or syrup   marshmallows or bananas, sliced

Boil potatoes until tender and peel, or take canned potatoes. Mash them, add sugar or syrup, fat, and salt, and mix well. Turn into greased baking dish, dot top with marshmallows or sliced bananas, and place in moderate oven long enough for marshmallows to swell and brown. Serve hot.

The recipes included directions for preparing lemonade for 150 people, 4 different kinds of toast ("Toast," "Crisped Crusts," "Water Toast," and "Milk Toast"), and such unusual dishes as "Frog Legs à la Newburg," "Fried Oysters," "Cracker Gruel," "Fried Mush," "Rhubarb Water," "Fried Smelts," "Goose Liver Patties," "Frozen Kiss Pudding," and "Mulligatawny (pepper and curry) Soup."

Advertisements were placed together at the beginning, middle, and end of the cookbook. The Boston Store, the Hotel Pfister, and the Plankinton House Hotel were among the advertisers. Ads for Milwaukee's finest foods featured Ambrosia Chocolate and Cocoa, Gebhardt's Confections (sweets), E. R. Pahl & Co. Pan Cake Flour, and Charles Ludwig's Hamburg Sausage.

E. R. Pahl & Co. Pan Cake Flour ad

WHI IMAGE ID 7467

PLACE FILE: MILWAUKEE.454

Hotel Pfister, about 1900-1910

Plankinton House Hotel

Hotels and food stores were some of the businesses that put ads in Lizzie's cookbook.

COURTESY MILWAUKEE COUNTY HISTORICAL SOCIETY

CHARLES LUDWIG,

Importer of and Dealer in

Hamburg, Holland, French and Norwegian.

Herring and Delicacies

Sausages, Cold Cuts and Appetizers

64 JUNEAU AVE.,   MILWAUKEE.

TELEPHONE MAIN 6213

The demand for copies of the sold-out first edition led to a second printing of 1,500 copies in 1903. Although Lizzie and her committee could have reprinted the first edition exactly as it had been originally printed, they didn't. They wanted to make an even better cookbook for the next edition.

9

Bigger and Better

What is in an astronaut's favorite sandwich?
Launch meat.

How do you make something good even better? Just as Lizzie continually made changes in the Settlement to better serve the needs of the community, she also edited and improved her cookbook. Lizzie carefully reread her copy of *The Settlement Cook Book*. She wrote comments on each page listing changes she wanted to make in the next edition. She changed the book's organization to make it easier to find recipes. She moved the index from the back to the front of the book. She combined "Recipes" and "Lessons in Cooking" into one section.

Lizzie corrected spelling errors from the first edition, added new recipes, and eliminated others. She included important information that had been missing from the

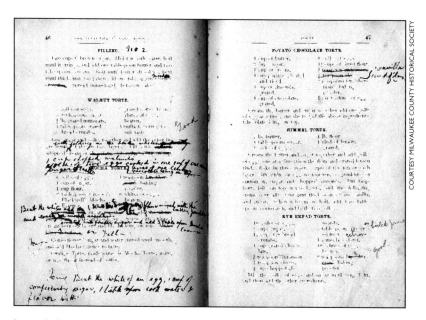

Lizzie's handwritten revisions from the 1901 edition

original edition, such as stating the amount of shrimp to use in the "Shrimp Spanish" recipe ("1 pint shrimp"). She tinkered with recipes, sometimes changing the quantities of certain ingredients. For example, she reduced the amount of curry powder used in "Curried Eggs" from one cup to one teaspoon. The new recipe for "Potato Chocolate Torte" used cinnamon instead of vanilla and the rind of a lemon instead of cloves. The 1903 edition also credited "Mrs. Simon Kander and Mrs. Henry Schoenfeld" for their help in collecting the recipes.

Imagine a World Without Broccoli

"I do not like broccoli. And I haven't since I was a little kid and my mother made me eat it. And I'm President of the United States and I'm not going to eat any more broccoli."

— George H. W. Bush, U.S. President, 1990

The word *broccoli* comes from the Italian word *brocco,* meaning arm branch. The first eighteen editions of *The Settlement Cook Book* included recipes for almost every vegetable commonly eaten today except broccoli. Why no broccoli? Although broccoli entered the United States in the 1700s, it didn't become popular until the 1920s, when Stephano and Andrea D'Arrigo planted broccoli in California and began shipping it to Boston. Meeting with success, they established their growing broccoli business with the brand name Andy Boy, named after Stephano's two-year-old son, Andrew.

By the 1930s, the country was having a love affair with broccoli. People were convinced that broccoli was a newly developed plant. Broccoli was still so new that the nineteenth edition (1931) of *The Settlement Cook Book* even included an explanation of what broccoli was and what it looked like: "Broccoli is a vegetable of the cabbage family. It has leafy stalks topped with flowerets which are best when dark green and buds are tightly closed. Wash well, cut off tough ends of stalks, [and] leave whole or cut into pieces. Steam, or cook in an open kettle in a large amount of boiling salted water *only* until tender. Drain and serve with hot butter, 'White Sauce,' page 120, or 'Hollandaise Sauce,' page 125."

So began the growth of the cookbook. The third edition, published 4 years later in 1907, was more than double the size of the second. "Household Rules" now included how "To Air a Room" ("Lower the upper sash of a window, to let out foul air, which always rises to the top...."). A new final chapter on preparing food for the sick, "**Invalid (in** vuh lid) Cooking," cautioned, "In preparing food for an invalid the following points should be kept in mind: The food should be served in the most pleasing manner possible. It should be suited to the digestive powers of the patient, and should be served in small quantities, just enough to satisfy hunger or to furnish needed strength...."

Recipes for "Turkish Pilaf," "Chop Suey," and "Spaghetti Italienne" gave the book a more international flavor. The expanded chapter on "Meats" included a new diagram of "Divisions and Ways of Cooking a Side of Beef" and new recipes for "Beef's Tongue," "Calf's Heart," and "Fried Goose Liver." The "Soups" chapter grew to include chicken, turkey, and goose soup.

invalid: someone who is sick or injured

In future editions, Lizzie continued to edit the book to improve recipes, added household hints, and included popular cooking trends. She even consulted with chemists in city hall. In the 1910 edition, she added advice for "Removing Stains," such as blood, grass, and ink stains. The 1924 edition addressed the

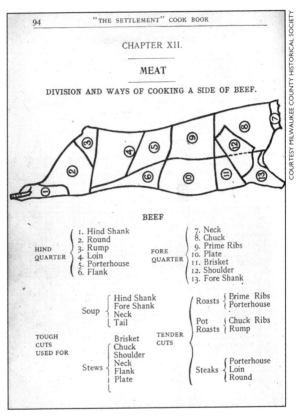

Diagram of a side of beef from the cookbook

growing popularity of household appliances by including directions for "Care of Vacuum Cleaners," "Care of the Electric Range," and "How to Regulate Oven Heat." In response to the popular trend of women buying baby foods from stores, a new section on "Infant Feeding" presented the daily recommended diets for babies from 6 to 9 months old and for children 2½ to 6 years old.

In 1925 Lizzie reported to the cookbook committee that *The Settlement Cook Book* was being used in China, Hawaii, Palestine, and Australia. The 1976 edition of *The Settlement Cook Book* was named to the James Beard "Cookbook Hall of Fame." By 1991 *The Settlement Cook Book* had gone through more than 40 editions and had sold more than 2 million copies. *The Settlement Cook Book* had become the most **profitable** (**prof** ih tuh buhl) charity cookbook ever published.

Why has Lizzie's "little venture" remained so popular for such a long time? In part, it's because Lizzie was a clear writer and a talented editor. She was also good at marketing, which means she got the word out that her cookbook was special and appealing.

Her original plan had been to create a textbook just for the Settlement's cooking classes. When Lizzie added recipes contributed by her friends, she more than doubled the number of women who would be interested in buying the book. By including both simple recipes for beginning cooks and more complicated recipes for experienced cooks,

profitable: producing a profit

74

the book appealed to immigrant women, who were new to American cooking, and to American women looking for new recipes to surprise and delight their families. Immigrant women could buy the book to learn to cook American dishes. American women could brag that Mrs. Kander had included *their* recipes in her cookbook. Indeed, it became quite an honor for a Milwaukee woman to be asked for a recipe to be included in a new edition.

Lizzie had a simple explanation for the popularity of her book:"The recipes are tested in my own kitchen. They are practical, economical, and reliable. The directions are given in simple language and easy to follow."

She insisted that every recipe be tested many times in her own kitchen and by committee members. She experimented with different ingredients and proportions until she was happy with the result. If she wasn't satisfied with a recipe after testing it, she wouldn't include it. She had friends and relatives try samples. Her husband Simon once asked her to "cut that pancake out of the **bill of fare** for at least a week"

bill of fare: menu

because she had served it to him so many times. All this repeated testing resulted in recipes that worked well and tasted good.

Although Lizzie was an experienced cook, she knew that her students were not. She used simple language in her cookbook to give inexperienced cooks a clear road map for preparing tasty and nutritious meals. She chose recipes that were short and easy to follow. These qualities made the book appealing to many immigrants still learning English,

For

Mr. & Mrs. Joe Futowsky: —

Here's wishing you both a long and useful life; a may this little book of min help keep you well and happy; for you well know "We may live without art; We may live without book But civilized man Can not live without Coon

Mrs. Simon Kander.

December, 1928.

Lizzie wrote her warm wishes in a gift copy of her cookbook.

to homemakers struggling to prepare good meals for their families, and to new brides. Not surprisingly, Lizzie's book remains a longtime favorite wedding-shower present for grandmothers, aunts, and mothers to give to young women. By giving Lizzie's cookbook as a gift, these women are sharing traditions with a younger generation.

The recipes came from the kitchens of Milwaukee and offered foods that people in Milwaukee wanted to eat. The old-fashioned German recipes appealed to Milwaukee's large German population, Jewish and non-Jewish alike. And the cookbook's focus on Jewish cooking made it especially attractive to Milwaukee's Jewish population. The cookbook interested Jewish women far beyond Milwaukee as well. Eventually, it became one of the best-known Jewish cookbooks in history!

Lizzie served as the main editor for each of the first 23 editions of *The Settlement Cook Book*. And since Lizzie kept the cookbook up-to-date with current tastes and food fads, it remained popular. When the Chinese board game mah-jongg became popular in the 1920s, Lizzie included a "Chinese Menu" in the cookbook. The 1934 edition contained one of the first descriptions in an American cookbook of Scandinavian **smorgasbord** (**smor** gus bord). Lizzie was so dedicated to improving the book that she continued testing new recipes until the day she died.

smorgasbord: a meal at which guests serve themselves from a table that consists of a variety of cold and hot foods

10

Chickens and Goats in the Playground

Why did the chicken cross the playground?
To get to the other slide.
Knock knock? Who's there? Goat. Goat who?
Goat to the door and find out.

Lizzie wanted to do more for the young people of
Milwaukee than just provide activities such as cooking and
sewing classes inside of the Settlement House. She turned
her attention to outdoor activities as well. In the early 1900s,
Milwaukee had only a few small playgrounds. In 1902,
Lizzie persuaded the School Board of Milwaukee to allow
the Settlement to open a playground on a vacant lot next
to the Sixth Street School (now called Golda Meir School).
Settlement House staff would supervise the playground since
it was believed that children needed playground supervision
at all times.

The new playground had a sand
pile, a canal filled with water for sailing
toy boats, a drinking fountain, a double
swing and several smaller swings, a tent,
a hammock, benches, butterfly nets,
and games such as croquet. Before the
playground opened, the neighborhood

children came to the Settlement every day and asked when
they could play on the playground.

When the playground officially opened on July 13, 1903,
The *Milwaukee Journal* described it as the "first adequately
equipped public playground in Milwaukee. It will be open
from 9 a.m. to 6 p.m. ….The playground will not be open in
the evening, as funds are not sufficient to provide a teacher to
supervise it at this time."

The playground was popular as soon as it opened,
although sometimes there were problems. In the spring
of 1906, for example, Lizzie had to ask the school board to
provide wire to prevent stray chickens, goats, and dogs from
wandering onto the playground. Within a year, the newly

formed Milwaukee Recreation Department took over the management of the playground from the Settlement House.

In 1907, Lizzie moved to Madison and attended classes at the University of Wisconsin while her husband Simon served in the state legislature. One day, she was called out of a class to answer a long-distance phone call. The call was from the women of the School Alliance in Milwaukee, who were asking her to run for election to the Milwaukee School Board. Lizzie, who was relieved that the call wasn't telling her that something was wrong at home, muttered, "Is that all—well— yes." She lost that election but was appointed to the school board later that year and served for the next 12 years.

Once she was a member of the school board, Lizzie began a campaign to open a girls' trade high school. In 1907, the Boys' Trade and Technical High School had opened to train young men in mechanical drawing, machine design, and plumbing. Lizzie wanted to open a similar school for girls that would offer classes in sewing, hatmaking, dressmaking, and cooking. She was upset when she learned that the men of the school board were more concerned about the education of boys than of girls.

It took Lizzie 18 months to persuade the board members to open the Girls' Trade School. She knew that she needed support from the community for her proposal to succeed. She received help from several female school principals, including 2 women who had been her classmates at East Side High School. Many of these women had visited Settlement House classes and adopted its teaching methods in their own schools. On March 2, 1909, 12 women principals sent a petition to the school board urging them to open a girls' trade school.

It took further female persuasion to convince the male members of the school board of the value of the project. Once Lizzie promised that the school would not allow any girl to graduate until she was able to make clothes for herself and her family and to prepare and serve meals properly, the board agreed to establish the Girls' Trade School.

The school opened in November 1909 with 53 girls. By 1941, some 1,800 girls had attended the school. Lizzie's clever planning and determination had made the school possible. For years, she delighted in wearing the clothes sewed for her by the students.

Lizzie's contributions to education also included helping Milwaukee's youngest children. In 1928, with funds from *The Settlement Cook Book*, she helped to establish the first nursery school in Milwaukee at the Milwaukee State Teachers College (now the University of Wisconsin–Milwaukee). Lizzie believed that having such a program at the teachers college would show the value of educating young children. She was right. After 2 experimental years, more nursery schools were established in Milwaukee and throughout Wisconsin. During World War II, many of these centers were able to stay open only because of funds they received from the Settlement Cook Book Fund.

The First 5 Kindergarteners in America

Did you attend kindergarten? If your answer is "yes," you have Margarethe Meyer Schurz to thank. She opened the first kindergarten class in the United States, in Watertown, Wisconsin.

Margarethe Schurz

Margarethe and her husband, Carl, left Germany to come to America in 1852. In Germany, Margarethe had been a student of Friedrich Froebel, the man who started the kindergarten idea in Germany. *Kindergarten* is a German word meaning "a garden where children grow." It was Froebel's idea to have a special classroom for beginning students. He believed that young children needed to have time to play in order to learn.

In 1856, after living in New York and Philadelphia, Margarethe and Carl moved to Watertown. Margarethe started a kindergarten in her home for her young daughter Agathe and 4 of her daughter's cousins. When more children wanted to join, Margarethe opened a school in a small building near their home. This was the first kindergarten in America.

Schooling in the 1800s was very strict. Student learning usually meant memorizing large amounts of information. The purpose of kindergarten was very different. Children in Margarethe Schurz's kindergarten learned by participating in activities with other children. They played games and sang songs and worked together in groups—much like students in kindergarten today. Each activity helped improve the young children's skills, but they also had great fun.

In 1859, Margarethe described her kindergarten to Elizabeth Peabody, a well-known writer and teacher. Peabody liked the idea very much, started the first kindergarten in St. Louis, and led a movement to establish kindergartens in other American communities. The rest, as they say, is history.

11

Abraham Lincoln and Lizzie

Where does Abraham Lincoln have his mail sent?
To his Gettysburg address.

"You should be ashamed," the father told his son.
"When Abraham Lincoln was your age, he used to walk 10 miles
every day to get to school." "Really?" the kid said.
"Well, when he was your age, he was president."

Almost from the moment it opened, the Settlement House needed additional space, as more and more people attended the classes and joined the clubs. In 1903, only 2 years after its opening, the Settlement moved to a larger building. But the landlord who owned the building forced the Settlement to move again in 1910. This time the Settlement Board of Directors decided that they wanted to buy their own building rather than rent someone else's.

Where would the needed $30,000 for the new building come from? Once again, Lizzie led the campaign to raise the money. She turned to the Settlement's most generous sponsors and cleverly found a way to win their help. Using recipes from her famous cookbook, Lizzie decided to prove that the way to a man's wallet (as well as to his heart) was through his stomach. She served a feast. The men ate to their hearts' delight, and by the end of the night, each man had contributed between $500 and $1,000 for the new building. This money, along with profits from cookbook sales, allowed the Settlement to buy land at 601 Ninth Street. By 1912, the new Settlement House opened.

Abraham Lincoln House
at 601 Ninth Street

MILWAUKEE URBAN ARCHIVES

The Board of Directors wanted to name the new building "Kander House" to thank Lizzie for her many accomplishments, but Lizzie refused the honor. She was modest and disliked public recognition. She received all the satisfaction she needed from doing the work she loved. Lizzie often commented that she benefited more than anyone else from her Settlement work because she learned so much from the immigrants.

Lizzie wanted the building to be named after Abraham Lincoln, the president she had always admired "as the great

Abraham Lincoln

American who was raised in even worse poverty than any of the immigrants." A building named after Lincoln would serve "as an inspiration to her hundreds of boys and girls." Thus, the Abraham Lincoln House was born, named after the president whose assassination had caused Lizzie's father to weep.

Like the Settlement House before it, the Abraham Lincoln House quickly grew in popularity. By 1922, the house newsletter, *The Lincoln News,* listed the following activities:

Boys	Girls	Adults
Athletic Clubs	Athletic Clubs	English Classes for Women
Educational Clubs	Educational Clubs	English Classes for Men
Scouts of America	Scouts	Mothers' Club
Game Room	Play Groups	Entertainments
Gymnastics	Dancing	Socials
Boxing	Dramatics	Library
Story Telling	Cooking	Club Work
Sketching	Sewing	Evening Classes in Jewish History
Dramatics	Piano Lessons	Dramatics
Music and Singing	Story Telling	Cooking
Entertainments	Hand Crafts	Sewing
Sabbath School	Entertainments	Music
	Sabbath School	Social Dancing
	Library	

In 1929, inadequate space became a problem again. The Abraham Lincoln House was sold. The money, together with profits from sales of *The Settlement Cook Book,* helped buy an even larger building, the University High School at 1025 N. Milwaukee Street. This building was remodeled and opened in 1931 with a new name: the Milwaukee Jewish Center. Later it was renamed the Jewish Community Center (JCC), a name it has carried into the twenty-first century. Lizzie became known as "The Mother of the Jewish Center."

Jewish Community Center

12

May I Have a Taste?

Why did the woman wear a helmet at the dinner table?
She was on a crash diet.

Lizzie wasn't content unless she was working on a project. When she gave up her seat on the school board in 1919 at the age of 62, she spent much of her time testing new recipes and making changes to *The Settlement Cook Book.* In 1920, Lizzie also organized the "Kitchen of Nations" for Milwaukee's Food, Household, and Electrical Show. This "Show of 1,000 Wonders" featured things used in the home including "food preparations, beverages, dairy products, furniture, musical instruments, [and] model dining rooms" that were sure to attract "the housewife, the college professor, the immigrant, and the businessman."

Lizzie at age 62

The Liquor Problem

Early editions of the *Settlement Cook Book* included several recipes containing alcohol, such as "Brandy Peaches," "Champagne Punch," and "Dandelion Wine." With the passage of the Eighteenth Amendment to the U.S. Constitution in 1919 (which prohibited selling and drinking alcohol), Lizzie and the Settlement Cook Book Committee had a problem. The cookbook contained recipes that now were illegal since they contained alcohol. They held an emergency meeting to figure out what to do. They decided to send a copy of the *Settlement Cook Book* to the attorney general of the United States to see what he suggested.

On February 1, 1920, John Kramer, **prohibition** commissioner, replied, "It is illegal to publish books after Jan. 17 containing instructions for the manufacture and use of liquor." As a result, the next 10 editions of the *Settlement Cook Book*, from 1920 to 1933, didn't have any recipes containing alcohol.

When Prohibition ended in 1933, a 16-page supplement to the *Settlement Cook Book* called "The Repeal Recipes" was published. It included the recipes containing alcohol that had been eliminated.

prohibition: the period (1920–1933) during which the Eighteenth Amendment to the U.S. Constitution forbidding the manufacture and sale of alcoholic beverages was the law in the United States

91

Sunday, October 10, 1920

Visitors to Milwaukee's Food, Household, and Electrical Show left with bags of free samples.

Lizzie's Kitchen of Nations turned out to be the most popular event at the food show. The kitchen featured foods prepared in kitchens from 15 different countries. Women dressed in folk costumes from each country cooked dishes such as "Polish **Borscht**" (borsht), "Oriental **Egg Foo Yong**" (egg foo **yuhng**), "Hungarian **Goulash**" (**goo** lahsh), "French **Crêpes**" (krapes), and "Italian Ravioli." The *Milwaukee Journal* reported that children flocked to the show because they received free samples, including breakfast cereals, nuts, and chewing gum.

The cooking demonstrations attracted huge crowds: "A drama in dough took place in the Hungarian kitchen. The word seemed to go round that the chubby bright-eyed **rotund** little cook there was about to put together a batch of apple

---

borscht: a beet soup from Russia or Poland   **egg foo yong:** a Chinese-American dish made by combining eggs with various foods such as bean sprouts, water chestnuts, scallions, ham, chicken, or pork
goulash: a stew made with meat (such as beef), assorted vegetables, and paprika   **crêpe:** very thin pancake
rotund: marked by roundness

strudel (stroo duhl) just what the women had all been reading about and wanted to see. The crowd gathered, fascinated and curious: 'What's she wrapping it in a cloth for?' 'It has to steam before she pulls

Cooks in the Hungarian kitchen made apple strudel for Lizzie's Kitchen of Nations.

it out.' 'It stretches like rubber and never breaks, does it?' ... Eventually, 'May I have a taste?' was the question on everyone's tongue as the long roll went into the oven."

Each kitchen promoted itself with a catchy slogan such as "Spaghetti, oh spaghetti, don't you forget it" (Italian kitchen) or "We eat to live, not live to eat" (French kitchen). Under Lizzie's leadership, the cooks presented nutritious, but low-cost, meals. The pamphlet of recipes printed from the food show, "Favorite Recipes of the Nations," sold for 10 cents. Part of the profits from the sales of tickets and pamphlets was donated to charity.

strudel: a pastry made from a thin sheet of dough rolled up with filling and baked

Lizzie's activities during the 1920s also included writing a cooking column for the *Milwaukee Journal*. For several years, her weekly column offered ideas for celebrating American holidays, including recipes, suggestions for decorations, sample invitations, and party activities, both for adults and for children.

Lizzie's column, which appeared in the *Milwaukee Journal* in the 1920s

---

• March 23, 1924 •

A Little Girl's Birthday Party

The birthday cake is the main attraction and should be placed in the center of the table. Make a huge sunshine cake, with pink frosting. Place yellow candles toward the center, have a border of small yellow candles. When the little guests have assembled, the host or hostess takes the hidden toys which the children have brought, and places them in a basket in the center of the living room. A circle is formed and one child at a time is blindfolded and is asked to take a package from the basket. No one is allowed to peep in. All they can do is smell and feel them. They are given 5 minutes in which they can exchange packages, as many times as they like, until they think they have something they really want. The mysterious packages are then opened, again exchanged if desired. The toys are now theirs to take home. The youngsters sit down on the floor and everybody entertains himself playing with his toy.

• March 30, 1924 •

An April Fool's Party
The invitation

Dear Tubby,

We are going to have an April Fool's Party at our home. Rig yourself up as foolish as you know how. Come about 5, stay until 9. We'll have eats. Girls are coming, too. Bet we'll have loads of fun!

• February 1924 •

A Luncheon for Washington's Birthday

Today we are planning a Washington's birthday party.... A picture of George Washington should have a conspicuous place in our room. Our Stars and Stripes, the Red, White and Blue, should radiate from every corner. A festive touch is added if your guests wear headdresses typical of Washington's time. The hostess should provide these: tricornered hats for the gentlemen and Martha Washington caps and kerchiefs for the ladies. These can be purchased or easily made of crepe paper. When inviting your guests ask them to make believe they were personal friends of George or Martha Washington and have them tell interesting or funny incidents in their visits and conversations with those 2 great personages. The one who tells the biggest "**whopper**" will be the prize winner. The menu includes recipes for "Virginia Corn Bread," "George Washington Cakes," and root beer floats called "Delaware Floats."

In 1940, Lizzie spent the early part of the summer in the hospital. She was such an active person that being sick bothered Lizzie less than being forced to rest while she recovered.

whopper: a big lie or a complex, made-up story

96

On July 24, shortly after returning home from the hospital, she received an order from Africa to buy *The Settlement Cook Book*. She telephoned her niece Irma to share her excitement about this news. She also told Irma that if the weather got cooler, she was going to cook one of the new recipes she'd recently received. Sadly, she never had a chance to try that recipe. Lizzie had a heart attack and died that same afternoon, at age 82.

Lizzie in her later years

Conclusion
A Twinkle in Her Eye

Why did the farmer win first place at the county fair?
Because she was outstanding in her field.

Photo of Lizzie that appeared in
The Settlement Cook Book

When the New York World's Fair of 1939 honored outstanding women from each state in the country, Lizzie Black Kander was chosen as one of the women to represent Wisconsin. The award was a tribute to her work helping the poor and needy for more than 60 years.

Lizzie represents all that was good and all that was complicated about the women of her day. She believed women's most important job was in the home, yet her most important contributions resulted from her work outside the home. She was a leader in organizations during a time when women rarely were in charge of anything beyond their households. She expected women to do what she said rather than what she did, but she served as a model for women who wanted to be active in their communities.

Perhaps it should not be surprising that Lizzie has influenced the decisions made daily in kitchens around the world. After all, she was the young woman who had confidently explained how she would solve America's problems "When I'm President." In her youth, she argued that women were best qualified for this task, and all through her life she devoted her energies to improving conditions in her community.

To her friends and family, Lizzie was a jolly, busy woman who would not let anybody wait on her or fuss over her. They recalled her kind, keen eyes, and the plump figure of her later years, which she laughingly claimed was due to good cooking from her own recipes.

"Everybody loved Mrs. Kander," stated Ardele Bok Kaplan, who knew Lizzie from the Jewish Community Center and smiled as she remembered her. Helen Krieg, Lizzie's housekeeper, said that Lizzie was so generous that "she would give her heart away." Lizzie's niece Irma recalled, "There always was a twinkle in her eye." Sarah Ettenheim, who served on the cookbook board with Lizzie, described her as "a person who is very determined—about almost anything. If you assigned her a task, you could be certain that she would stay with it until it was completed."

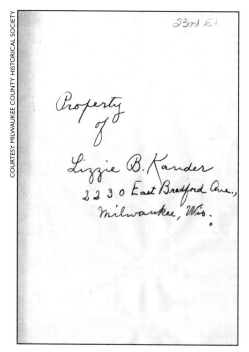

Lizzie's signature from the twenty-third edition

When Irma became engaged and married in 1916, Lizzie advised: "Like to do what you have to do, but do what you like to do." Lizzie spent most of her life doing what she liked to do. The world is a richer and tastier place because she did.

Afterword

Making a Positive Difference

In her day, Lizzie improved the lives of countless children and families in Milwaukee. She believed that everyone has a right to good food shared at a table with loved ones, to a good education, and to cleanliness that helps people stay healthy. Lizzie spent her entire adult life working to meet these basic needs of her neighbors. Today, her legacy lives on, with her *Settlement Cookbook* still earning money that helps women and children through the Greater Milwaukee Foundation.

Sadly, more than 100 years after Lizzie created her cookbook, there are still children in the world who don't have enough to eat, who can't go to school, and who don't have a place to live, so it's hard for them to stay clean and healthy. Lizzie Kander saw sad and unfair conditions around her, and used her talents to improve them. If she were here today, she would encourage us to work in our communities to make them better places to live.

Appendix

Lizzie's Time Line

1844 – Lizzie's parents, John and Mary Black, move to Milwaukee from a small farm in Green Bay, Wisconsin.

1858 – Lizzie is born in Milwaukee on May 28.

1861 – Lizzie is 3 years old when Abraham Lincoln becomes the sixteenth president of the United States.

1862 – Lizzie is 4 years old and is one of the first girls to attend the Fifth Ward School.

1865 – President Abraham Lincoln is assassinated on April 14, just 5 days after the Civil War ended.

1875 – Lizzie is in eighth grade and passes an exam required by the City of Milwaukee in order to advance to high school.

1878 – Lizzie graduates from Milwaukee's East Side High School. Her class elects her class valedictorian, so she speaks at the graduation ceremony.

1881 – Lizzie is 23 years old and very involved in volunteer work to help the poor immigrants of Milwaukee. On May 17, she marries Simon Kander.

1890 — Lizzie becomes a truant officer for the South Side School Alliance and begins visiting the homes of Milwaukee's immigrant families to find out why their children are not attending school.

1895 — While president of the Ladies Relief Sewing Society, Lizzie donates $75 to form the "Keep Clean Mission" to see that Milwaukee's poor children keep clean and are regularly sent to school.

1896 — The name of the "Keep Clean Mission" is changed to the "Milwaukee Jewish Mission."

1898 — The Milwaukee Jewish Mission is offering cooking classes for girls from ages 13 to 15, taught by volunteers including Lizzie.

1900 — The Milwaukee Jewish Mission combines with another Jewish charity, the Sisterhood of Personal Service, to form "The Settlement." Lizzie is chosen to be its first president, a position she holds for 18 years.

1900 — At least 17,000 people take baths in the first year of the Settlement's bathhouse.

1901 — Lizzie suggests to the Settlement's Cooking Committee that they publish a cookbook. The first edition of *The Settlement Cook Book: The Way to a Man's Heart* is published.

1903 – The demand for the sold-out first edition of
The Settlement Cook Book is so great that there is a second
printing of 1,500 copies.

1907 – The third edition of *The Settlement Cook Book* is published.
It is more than double the size of the second edition and
includes new recipes for marshmallows.

Lizzie temporarily moves to Madison and attends classes
at the University of Wisconsin while her husband serves in
the state legislature. Upon returning to Milwaukee,
she is appointed to the Milwaukee school board.

1909 – The Girls' Trade School, which Lizzie fought to get
established, opens in November with 53 students.

1910 – Another edition of *The Settlement Cook Book* is published.
Lizzie adds advice for removing stains.

1912 – The new Settlement House opens. Lizzie asks that it be
named after Abraham Lincoln.

1920 – Lizzie organizes the "Kitchen of Nations" for Milwaukee's
Food, Household, and Electrical Show.

1920s – Lizzie writes a cooking column for the *Milwaukee Journal.*

1925 – Lizzie reports to the cookbook committee that
The Settlement Cook Book is being used in China, Hawaii,
Palestine, and Australia.

1928 – Lizzie helps establish the first nursery school in Milwaukee.

1929 – The Abraham Lincoln House is sold to buy an even larger building, which opens in 1931 and is called the Milwaukee Jewish Center, later renamed what it is still called today, the Jewish Community Center.

1940 – Lizzie has a heart attack and dies on July 24, at age 82.

1976 – This year's edition of *The Settlement Cook Book* is named to the James Beard "Cookbook Hall of Fame."

1991 – *The New Settlement Cook Book,* now edited by a man, has gone through more than 40 editions, has sold more than 2 million copies, and is the most profitable charity cookbook ever published.

Recipes

The best part of a cookbook is its recipes. What follows is a sampling of recipes from Lizzie's *Settlement Cook Book*, from one of the earliest editions published in 1903 to one published 90 years later, in 1991.

1903 Edition

Spiced Cookies No. 1

5 whole eggs	1 teaspoon vanilla
1 pound brown sugar	1 teaspoon ginger
2 teaspoons cinammon	1 teaspoon baking soda
1 teaspoon ground cloves	Flour to roll

Mix the above together, add enough flour to handle it, roll into small balls, and bake on greased pans.

Frozen Chocolate Pudding

3 yolks	¼ cup sugar
¼ pound chocolate	1 pint whipped cream
½ cup milk	

Melt chocolate, sugar, and milk, add yolks of 3 eggs, well beaten, and when cooled, add to the cream. Freeze 3 hours.

The Way
To a....
Man's
Heart

"The Settlement"
Cook Book.

Milwaukee,
WIS.

Doughnuts

1 pint flour
½ pint sugar
1 teaspoon salt
2 teaspoons baking powder
1 egg

¼ teaspoon cinammon
A little grated nutmeg
2 tablespoons melted butter
½ cup milk

Sift dry ingredients. Add the milk to the beaten egg, and combine the mixtures. Roll on well floured board, cut with form, or roll into small balls, and fry in deep fat. Dust with powdered sugar.

Cracker or Matzos Balls

Butter size of walnut
Chopped parsley
1 egg
Salt and cracker meal

Stir the butter, add egg, then as much cracker meal as it absorbs. Moisten with a little soup, add parsley and salt. Roll into marbles and boil in the soup just before serving.

Cracker Gruel

4 tablespoons powdered cracker crumbs
1 cup boiling water
1 cup milk
½ teaspoon salt

Boil up once and serve.

Lemonade for 150 People

5 dozen lemons, squeezed | 1 dozen oranges, sliced
1 can or a fresh pineapple | 6 pounds sugar
6 gallons water | Ice

The rule is one pound of sugar for every dozen of fruit. If pineapple is fresh, add one more pound of sugar. Mix sugar with fruit and juice, and let stand. When ready to serve add water and ice, to keep cool.

Note: The sugar and some water may be boiled to a syrup, allowed to cool, and the fruit and juices added afterward.

1947 Edition

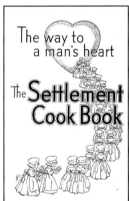

Kuchen Dough No. 1

1 pint scalded milk | 6 cups flour
½ cup butter | 1 egg or 2 egg yolks
¾ cup sugar | 1 cake compressed yeast
1 teaspoon salt | Grated rind of ½ lemon

Warm bowl and flour. Crumble the yeast in a cup with a teaspoon of sugar, and ½ cup of scalded milk cooled until lukewarm. Let stand in a warm place to rise.

To the rest of the scalded milk add the butter, sugar, salt, a little nutmeg, grated lemon, and when lukewarm, the beaten yolks of the 2 eggs; stir in the yeast and some flour, only enough more to knead, until smooth and elastic. Cover closely and let rise double its bulk.

Cut dough, form into any desired shape, place in pans, let rise again until double its size, and bake.

1965 Edition

Sauerbraten

4 pounds beef, chuck, rump, or round
Salt and pepper
1 onion, sliced
3 bay leaves
1 teaspoon whole peppercorns
Vinegar and water
Salt and sugar
¼ cup brown sugar
¼ cup raisins
4 to 6 gingersnaps

Sprinkle meat well with salt and pepper, and rub in thoroughly. Place meat with onion, bay leaves, and peppercorns in deep earthenware dish. Heat water and vinegar (equal parts if vinegar is very strong), and add salt and sugar to taste. Pour hot over meat to cover.

Cover dish well, refrigerate, and let stand 3 to 4 days, turning occasionally.

Put meat in kettle, add the onion slices and a little of the spiced vinegar, place in hot oven, 400 degrees, to brown. Cover tightly, reduce heat to moderately slow, and cook slowly about 3 hours, or until tender. Add more of the vinegar if necessary. Take out the meat, slice for serving, and keep hot. Strain liquid in kettle, skim off fat. Melt ¼ cup brown sugar in an iron skillet, add the strained liquid very gradually, then the raisins and gingersnaps. Cook until thickened and smooth and pour hot sauce over meat.

Or follow method for marinating meat, and brown meat in 2 tablespoons fat in a Dutch oven. Add small amount of the spiced vinegar, cover tightly, simmer slowly until tender, adding the spiced vinegar from time to time until all has been used. When ready to serve, strain the liquid, thicken with flour to make a brown gravy, adding sour cream, if desired.

1991 Edition

Hot Bacon and Peanut Butter Sandwiches
(also in 1947)

Cut wheat bread lengthwise into ¼-inch slices. Toast on one side. Spread untoasted side with a thick layer of peanut butter. Sprinkle top with crumbled crisp bacon. Before serving put under broiler to heat thoroughly. Cut into strips and serve.

Chewy Brownies

½ cup butter
2 ounces unsweetened chocolate, melted,
   or 6 tablespoons cocoa
1 cup sugar
2 eggs
½ cup flour
½ teaspoon vanilla
1 cup chopped walnuts
¼ teaspoon salt

Preheat oven to 350 degrees. Cream butter and sugar well. Beat in eggs one at a time. Add remaining ingredients.

Bake in a greased 8-inch square pan for 20 to 30 minutes. Cut into squares when cool.

Makes 12 to 15 brownies.

Muerbe (Basic Butter Cookies)

1 pound (2 cups **or** 4 sticks) butter
1¼ cups sugar (divided)
2 eggs, separated
½ teaspoon finely grated lemon rind
2 tablespoons lemon juice or brandy
6 cups flour
1 teaspoon baking powder
1 cup almonds, finely chopped

Cream butter, add 1 cup of the sugar and beat until light. Lightly beat egg yolks and add along with lemon rind, lemon juice or brandy, and the flour mixed with baking powder. Mix until all ingredients are well combined. Gather dough together in one lump, cover in plastic wrap, and chill for 2 hours.

Preheat oven to 350 degrees. On lightly floured board, roll out ½ of the dough at a time to a sheet ⅛ inch thick. Cut into desired shapes. Lightly beat egg whites and brush on the tops of the cookies. Sprinkle cookies with remaining ¼ cup sugar and the almonds.

Bake on greased cookie sheets for 10 to 15 minutes.

Makes about 80 small cookies.

Glossary

agency (**ay** jen see): office or business that provides services to the public

anti-Semitism (an tee **sem** ih tiz uhm): hatred of and discrimination against Jews

assassinated (us **sass** uh nay ted): killed, usually someone who is well-known

borscht (borsht): a beet soup from Russia or Poland

bib and tucker: best clothes

bile: a green liquid that is made by the liver and helps digest food

bill of fare: menu

chatelaine (sha tu **len**): old fashioned chain worn at the waist by women for carrying keys or purses

commitment: promise to do something or support something

contaminating: making unclean

corresponding: matching or going along with in some way

crêpe (krape): very thin pancake

crocheting (kro **shay** ing): using a special hooked needle to make a kind of needlework from thread or yarn

darn: to repair clothing by sewing crossed stitches very close together

demonstrated: showed something by doing it

disinfectant (dis in **fek** tant): a substance that destroys germs

dissected: cut open for study

drilling: exercises designed to develop a skill, such as marching in complicated formations like bands do at football games

dry goods store: general store that sold a variety of items like dry foods such as sugar and flour and cloth

dunce cap: cone-shaped paper cap that misbehaving students were forced to wear in the classroom as punishment. Also called fool's cap.

egg foo yong (egg foo **yuhng**): a Chinese-American dish made by combining eggs with various foods such as bean sprouts, water chestnuts, scallions, ham, chicken, or pork

embroidering (em **broy** dur ing): sewing a picture or design onto cloth

fund-raising: collecting money for a specific cause

garment: item of clothing

gastric: to do with the stomach

gefilte (guh **fel** tuh) **fish:** ground fish filled with seasoning, served cold

gelatin: a clear substance used in making jelly, desserts, and glue that is obtained from animal bones and tissue

globule: tiny ball, especially of liquid

goulash (goo lahsh): a stew made with meat (such as beef), assorted vegetables, and paprika

hasen pfeffer (hah ssen feff ur): marinated rabbit

home economics: science and art of managing a household

immigrant: someone who leaves a country to permanently live in another country

influence: to have an effect on someone or something

intestinal: having to do with the intestine, a long tube extending below the stomach that digests food and absorbs liquids and salts; it consists of the small intestine and the large intestine

invalid (in vuh lid): someone who is sick or injured

kosher (koh shur): food prepared according to Jewish dietary laws

kuchen (kuk ken): coffee cake

kugel (koo gull): baked noodle pudding

matzah (maht zuh) **ball:** dumpling-like ball made of matzah meal, eggs, and oil, boiled in chicken soup

needy: very poor

nursery: a place where babies and very young children are looked after while their parents are at work

nutritious (noo **trish** uhss): food containing substances that your body can use to help you stay strong and healthy

pancreatic (pan kree at ik): having to do the with the pancreas, a gland near the stomach that makes a fluid to help digest food

pawn: person or thing used to get something or gain an advantage

persecuted (pur suh **kyoo** tud): treated cruelly and unfairly because of religion or beliefs

pfeffernusse (feff ur nooss): holiday cookie

pledge: promise to donate money

poverty (pov ur tee): being poor

profitable (prof ih tuh buhl): producing a profit

prohibition: the period (1920-1933) during which the Eighteenth Amendment to the U.S. Constitution forbidding the manufacture and sale of alcoholic beverages was the law in the United States

prominent: famous or important

proteid (pro teed): protein

ration (rash un): food supply

resolution (rez uh **loo** shun): a course of action decided on by a meeting; agreed to by a vote

rotund: marked by roundness

satire (sat ire): humorous criticism

smorgasbord (smor gus bord): a meal at which guests serve themselves from a table that consists of a variety of cold and hot foods

spectator: someone who watches an event and does not participate in it

stout: quite fat; large and heavily built

strudel (stroo duhl): a pastry made from a thin sheet of dough rolled up with filling and baked

suffrage (suf ridj): the right to vote in an election

suitable: right for a particular purpose

tact: being sensitive to people and not upsetting or hurting anyone's feelings

tenement (ten uh ment): home for the poor, often in run-down condition

thrifty: careful with money

torte (tort): cake in which ground nuts or crumbs are usually used instead of flour

truant officer: someone who finds children who do not show up for school

valedictorian (val uh dik **tor** ee uhn): the student, usually with the highest grades in the class, who speaks at graduation

venture: a project that is somewhat risky, as in a business venture

wage: the money someone is paid for his or her work

whopper: a big lie or a complex, made-up story

Reading Group Guide and Activities

Discussion Questions

Introduction Through Conclusion

❧ Author Bob Kann begins each section or chapter of the book with a joke or riddle that relates to the material in that section. Read the jokes and discuss how each one relates to the text.

Chapter 1

❧ Read about how Lizzie and her brothers and sisters had fun growing up in the 1860s and compare it to the things you do with your free time.

❧ Lizzie's mother trained her daughters for marriage and homemaking. What were some of the things she expected them to know? Why do you think such training was important to Lizzie's mother? How do you think Lizzie felt about her mother's wishes? What is your mother or father training you to become? How do you feel about it?

❧ Look at the "A Really Difficult Exam" sidebar and test yourself on some of the questions. Which are the hardest questions for you to answer? Do you think they might have been easier to answer if you had lived 100 years ago? Why?

Chapter 2

Read about Lizzie's graduation speech and think about what you would do if you were the president of the United States. How do you think your goals would be different from those Lizzie wanted to accomplish?

Chapter 3

Lizzie's family were all German Jews. She had mixed feelings about the Russian Jews moving into Milwaukee. What kinds of things did she do to help these new immigrants? How do you think her actions helped her handle her feelings? How would you feel if your cousins from another country moved into your neighborhood? What would you think if you'd never met them before and they wore different clothes, spoke a different language, and behaved differently from you? Would you welcome them and help them to fit in? If yes, how would you do this? What might some of the problems be? How do you think you would deal with them?

Chapter 4

In the late 1800s, sewing and cooking were important skills for girls to possess. In what ways are they important today? Are they important only for girls? What are important skills for girls and for boys to possess today? Which skills might be more important for girls? Why? Which skills might be more important for boys? Why?

Chapter 8

❧ Read about the hasen pfeffer, pfeffernusse, and other ethnic recipes that Lizzie put in *The Settlement Cookbook* and talk about some of the traditional family recipes you have at your house. Are there special foods you have on holidays? What are some of your favorites? What are some you don't like?

❧ Lizzie believed that "a way to a man's heart" was through good cooking. What are special foods in your family that are "ways" to someone's heart? Describe a family occasion where food is important. Why do you think people often associate certain foods with happy times?

Chapter 10

❧ Read the "The First 5 Kindergarteners in America"section. Do you remember your first day? What were some of your favorite experiences in kindergarten? Why do you think you remember them so fondly? Why do you suppose we remember some things, even from a long time ago, and not others? Do you feel strongly— happy or upset—about many of your clearest memories?

Chapter 12

❧ Read Lizzie's party plans for a February 17, 1924, luncheon for President Washington's birthday and come up with a big whopper (a big lie or a complex, made-up story). Write it down and exchange whoppers with others in your reading group or class. What kinds of things make a prize-winning whopper?

Conclusion

 Lizzie was unusual for a woman of her time because of her abilities to organize and make changes outside of the home. What personal strengths helped her achieve her goals? What kinds of things do you want to accomplish? What kinds of strengths can you use to achieve your dreams?

Activities and Projects

 Call a local food pantry and find out what kinds of food are most needed. Organize a collection drive in your community.

 Try some of the recipes in the Appendix and see which ones are your favorites. Organize a favorite recipe exchange with others in your reading group or class.

 Pick out a bunch of questions in the "Really Difficult Exam" from Chapter 1 and see if you can answer them. If you can't, see if you can find the answers in books or on the Internet.

Acknowledgments

If it takes a village to raise a child, I learned that it also takes a mini-village to write a book. As someone who spends most of my time telling stories, I found that writing them presented very different and often difficult challenges. I am fortunate to have friends and family members whose suggestions on my early drafts of this book made me feel better and more confident about the entire enterprise. Thank you to all of the following:

Deborah Waxman for once again taking my words and making them more precise and grammatically accurate. Caroline Hoffman showed me how to make the leap from writing for adults to writing for kids. Judy Landsman helped to make this book even more readable for kids. Shayle Kann asked good questions and, like his mother, listened to my stories and enthusiasm about Lizzie. Bobbie Malone provided me with the opportunity to write this book and the privilege of working with the Wisconsin Historical Society. She also shared her editorial wisdom and enthusiasm about Lizzie. Erica Schock and Deborah Johnson worked with Bobbie to "put it all together." Others at the Society were indispensable in making this book a reality. Elizabeth Boone managed its production and engaged the able assistance of Brian Bengston, Joel Heiman, Joe Kapler, John Nondorf, and John Zimm. Special thanks also goes to the talented designers: Nancy Zucker for the cover and Jill Bremigan for the interior pages.

Several historians of food- and cooking-related subjects throughout the United States generously answered my questions or told me where to look for the answers. Librarians at the Wisconsin Historical Society, Milwaukee County Historical Society, and Milwaukee Jewish Historical Society provided me with invaluable help researching the life of Lizzie Kander and trying to understand how the world worked more than 100 years ago. Just as Lizzie's community helped her to write her book, my community helped me to write this book.

Index

Note: This index points to the pages where you can read about persons, places, and ideas. When you see a **boldface** page number, it means there is a picture or a map on the page.

If you do not find the word you are looking for, try to think of another word that means about the same thing. Sometimes the index will point to another word, like this: Schools, *see also* education.

If you are looking for Lizzie's recipes, check the Recipe Index on page 127.

H

Housekeeping, 59, 72
Hygiene. *See* cleanliness

I

Immigrants. *See* Jewish immigrants

J

Jewish Community Center, 89, **89**
Jewish immigrants
    anti-Semitism, 24
    food and fitting into American
    culture, 54–55
    Lizzie's work to help, 23–24
    maps showing home countries of, *xi*,
    22
    with meat market, **45**
    needs of, 21–25
    reasons for coming to America,
    21–22, 24
Jokes and riddles
    Abraham Lincoln in, 85
    astronauts in, 69
    bees in, 1
    chickens in, 78
    doctors in, 38
    elephants in, 20, 64
    fairies in, 27
    food in, 44, 50, 54, 58, 64, 69, 90
    frogs in, 20
    germs in, 31
    knock-knocks, 78
    light bulbs in, *ix*
    octopuses in, 38
    porcupines in, 1

presidents in, 14, 85
    sewing in, 20
    vegetables in, 38
Joseph Schlitz Brewing Company, **36**
Judaism
    anti-Semitism, 24
    social responsibility and, 12
    See also Jewish immigrants

K

Kander, Elizabeth "Lizzie" Black, **21, 28,
48, 56, 57, 90, 97, 98**
    death of, 96–97
    as fund-raiser, *x*, 40–41, 51–53, 82, 86
    marriage to Simon Kander, 27–29
    as newspaper columnist, 94–96
    as teacher, *x–xii,* 49
    as truant officer, 29–30
Kander, Simon, 27–29, **28**, 40, **56**, 75, 80
Kaplan, Ardele Bok, 100
"Keep Clean Mission," 30, 33, 36
"Kitchen of Nations" exhibit, 90, 92–93,
93
Krieg, Helen, 100

L

Ladies Relief Sewing Society, 25, 30
Lincoln, Abraham, **11,** 11–12, 87, **87**

M

Marshmallows, 63–65
Milwaukee Jewish Mission
    games and playing at, 33
    "Keep Clean Mission" as early form

Recipe Index